Sushi Cookbook

The Step-by-Step Sushi Guide for beginners with easy to follow, healthy, and Tasty recipes. How to Make Sushi at Home Enjoying 101 Easy Sushi and Sashimi Recipes. Your Sushi Made Simple!

© Copyright 2019 - All rights reserved.

The content contained within this book may not be reproduced, duplicated or transmitted without direct written permission from the author or the publisher.

Under no circumstances will any blame or legal responsibility be held against the publisher, or author, for any damages, reparation, or monetary loss due to the information contained within this book, either directly or indirectly.

Legal Notice:

This book is copyright protected. It is only for personal use. You cannot amend, distribute, sell, use, quote or paraphrase any part, or the content within this book, without the consent of the author or publisher.

Disclaimer Notice:

Please note the information contained within this document is for educational and entertainment purposes only. All effort has been executed to present accurate, up to date, reliable, complete information. No warranties of any kind are declared or implied. Readers acknowledge that the author is not engaged in the rendering of legal, financial, medical or professional advice.

Table of contents

- **Introduction**..8

- **Essential Tools and Ingredients for Sushi Making** 18

- **Sushi Soup & Salad Recipes**..21
  - *1*-Healthy Sushi Salad
  - *2*-Veggie Sushi Roll Salad
  - *3*-Simple Sushi Salad
  - *4*-Shrimp Sushi Salad
  - *5*-Simple Sushi Rice Salad
  - *6*-Sushi Shiso Salad
  - *7*-Sushi Salad with Sauce
  - *8*-Sushi Salmon Salad
  - *9*-Sushi Rice Soup
  - *10*-Miso soup

- *Did You Know?*..36

- **Vegetable Sushi Recipes**..37
  - *11*- Avocado Cauliflower Sushi
  - *12*- Avocado Peanut Sushi
  - *13*- Avocado Cucumber Sushi
  - *14*- Avocado Cream Cheese Sushi
  - *15*- Simple Wasabi Cucumber Avocado Sushi
  - *16*- Healthy Cucumber Avocado Sushi Roll
  - *17*- Bell Pepper Avocado Sushi Roll

- 18- *Avocado Cucumber Zucchini Sushi Rolls*
- 19- *Lentil Vegetable Sushi Healthy*
- 20- *Veggie Sushi Rolls*
- 21- *Pear Cucumber Sushi*
- 22- *Healthy Vegetarian Sushi*
- 23- *Vegetable Quinoa Sushi Rolls*
- 24- *Asian Sushi Rolls*
- 25- *Veggie Cream Cheese Sushi*
- 26- *Sweet Potato Sushi*
- 27- *Miso Carrot Sushi*
- 28- *Cucumber Mango Sushi*
- 29- *Mix Vegetable Sushi*

❖ **Did You Know?**..64

❖ **Meat And Egg Sushi Recipes**..66

- 30- *Delicious Chicken Sushi*
- 31- *Spicy Chicken Sushi*
- 32- *Fried Chicken Sushi Rolls*
- 33- *Teriyaki Beef Sushi*
- 34- *Sweet and Spicy Chicken Sushi*
- 35- *Yummy Chicken Schnitzel Sushi Rolls*
- 36- *Brown Rice Chicken Sushi Rolls*
- 37- *Egg Chicken Sushi Rolls*
- 38- *Veggie Chicken Sushi Rolls*
- 39- *Ham Egg Sushi*
- 40- *Egg Omelet Nigiri*
- 41- *Pesto Egg Sushi*
- 42- *Edamame Egg Sushi*
- 43- *Egg Avocado Sushi Rolls*
- 44- *Egg Smoked Salmon Sushi Rolls*

❖ **Did You Know?**..87

❖ *Tofu Sushi Recipes*..89

- *45- Spicy Vegetable Tofu Sushi Rolls*
- *46- Tofu Sushi Rolls*
- *47- Vegetable Tofu Sushi*
- *48- Spicy Tofu Sushi*
- *49- Smoky Tofu Sushi*
- *50- Fried Tofu Sushi*
- *51-Healthy Vegan Sushi Rolls*
- *52- Asparagus Tofu Sushi Rolls*
- *53- Quinoa Tofu Sushi Rolls*
- *54- Tofu Brown Rice Sushi Rolls*
- *55- Smoked Tofu Avocado Sushi Rolls*

❖ *Did You Know?*..106

❖ *Seafood Sushi Recipes*..108

- *56- Salmon Sushi Rolls*
- *57- Smoked Salmon Sushi Rolls*
- *58- Tuna Sushi Roll*
- *59- Salmon Cauliflower Sushi Rolls*
- *60- Salmon Cream Cheese Sushi roll*
- *61- Salmon Sriracha Sushi Rolls*
- *62- Canned Tuna Sushi Rolls*
- *63-Asparagus Crab Sushi Rolls*
- *64-Spicy Cauliflower Tuna Sushi Rolls*
- *65-Delicious Shrimp Sushi Rolls*
- *66-Spicy Tuna Sushi Rolls*
- *67-Salmon Sushi Roll*
- *68-Cucumber Salmon Sushi*
- *69-Tuna Teriyaki Rolls*
- *70-Salmon Cream Cheese Roll*
- *71-Delicious Sashimi Tuna Roll*
- *72-Shrimp Avocado Sushi*
- *73- Crab Meat Sushi*
- *74- Easy Cucumber Crabmeat Sushi*
- *75-Flavorful Tuna Sushi Rolls*

- ❖ **Did You Know?**..135

- ❖ **Sashimi Recipes**..137
  - 76- Miso Soy Tuna Sashimi
  - 77- Chive Soy Tuna Sashimi
  - 78- Salmon Sashimi
  - 79- Ginger Salmon Sashimi
  - 80- Healthy Tuna Sashimi
  - 81- Sea Bass Sashimi
  - 82- Delicious Tuna Sashimi

- ❖ **Did You Know?**..148

- ❖ **Nigiri Sushi**..150
  - 83- Fresh Tuna Nigiri Sush
  - 84- Salmon Nigiri Sushi
  - 85- Shrimp Nigiri
  - 86- Scallop Nigiri
  - 87- Avocado Nigiri
  - 88- Tasty Hamachi Nigiri
  - 89- Cucumber Nigiri
  - 90- Healthy Carrot Nigiri

- ❖ **Did You Know?**..163

- ❖ **Dessert Sushi Recipes**...164
- 91- Yummy Banana Nutella Sushi Roll
- 92- Chocolate Fruit Sushi Rolls
- 93- Fresh Fruit Sushi Rolls
- 94- Banana Nuts Sushi
- 95- Sweet and Spicy Grapefruit Sushi Rolls
- 96- Chia Honey Banana Sushi Rolls
- 97- Yummy Mango Sushi
- 98- Gluten Free Chocó Oats Banana Sushi

- *99- Yummy Strawberry Jam Sushi*
- *100- Chocolate Walnut Banana Sushi*
- *101- Pineapple Cantaloupe Strawberry Sushi Rolls*

LET'S START!!!

Preface

Sushi is the traditional Japanese way of cooking food that includes serving seasoned rice in a combination of fish, seafood, vegetables, meat, fruits and other ingredients. Sushi is extremely versatile and offers an impressive variety of colorful flavors. The cuisine originated in the East, but today it is extremely popular food in the West. Preparing sushi doesn't require a lot of effort and patience.

With the help of this beginner's sushi making guide, start to make this delicious food at your home today. Often people think making sushi is a delicate art and can't be achieved by amateurs. However, this book will clarify and explain the sushi preparation techniques and make sushi making fun and enjoyable for a beginner like you. The book will show how easy it is to make sushi even for people who are not familiar with Japanese cuisine.

The book offers practical sushi preparation guidance with a friendly voice. With this beginner's sushi guide, enjoy one of the world's healthiest and most palate-pleasing cuisines in the comfort of your own home. Sushi can be an inquired taste for food lovers, so this book gives you a wide variety of sushi recipes including vegetarian, sushi salad, fish, seafood, meat, and even dessert sushi recipes. So why wait, gather some quality sushi grade ingredients, buy a rolling mat, and start to make some sushi.

Introduction

Delicious and healthy, sushi is for anyone who loves to eat healthily and enjoy serving special  meals to friends and family on special occasions, birthdays or during any family event. This complete book on sushi for beginners provides all the important information you need to get started on sushi making. You only need a few simple tools and sushi grade cooking materials, and you can start making a wide variety of delicious sushi recipes.

Essential Tools and Ingredients for Sushi Making

Let's discuss the essential tools and equipment's you need to make sushi at your home. Here are 7 essential tools that will help you master sushi:

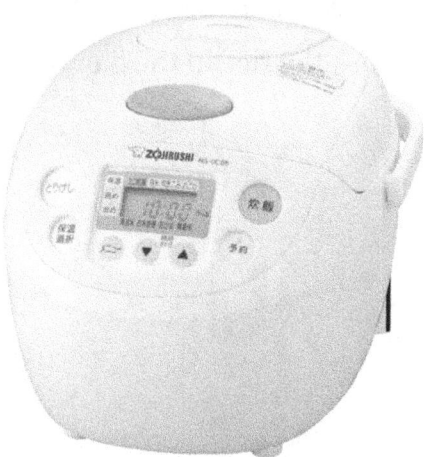

1. A Suihanki: Perfectly cooked rice is an essential element of good sushi. Professional Japanese sushi restaurants use shank or a rice cooker.

2. Hangiri: Once the rice is cooked, you need a bowl to place it, and then add sugar, salt, and vinegar. A wooden container known as hangiri is the best choice.

3. Shamoji: You have to mix the cooked rice with a rice paddle, so excess moisture probate and rice are ideal for making sushi. Shamoji is ideal when you need to work the rice in the hangiri.

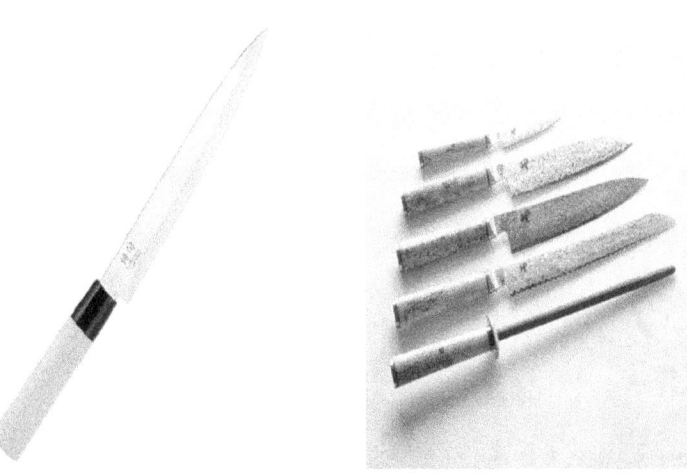

4. The Knife: You need a knife for sushi. It is even better if you own a set of sushi knives. For a beginner sushi maker, the above knife will do.

5. The Sharpening Stone: Your knives need to be sharp for proper sushi cuts. You need a sharping stone like the above to keep your knives sharp.

6. The Makisu: Before cutting them, you need to roll beautiful California and maki rolls. The bamboo mat known as makisu is the tool you need for it.

7. The presentation: To get authenticity to the dish and follow the Japanese sushi tradition, you need these.

We discussed the tools that you need. Now discuss the ingredients that you need:

Sushi Rice (Sushi –Meshi)

Good quality sushi rice is important to make top quality sushi because sushi rice is the foundation of the sushi. You need to choose the best rice, then wash it, soak it and then cook accordingly.

Rice Vinegar (Gomez)

With cooked rice, you need to mix a combination of salt, sugar and rice vinegar to give it that sweet and tart flavor. You can find good quality rice vinegar at Amazon or in your local Japanese grocery store.

Kombu

Kombu is a must ingredient to make the very best sushi rice for your sushi. Kombu gives the rice that hint of dashi flavor. You need to place it in the rice cooker during the rice soaking and cooking period.

Sake

Along with kombu, sake is also important. It also gives the rice a hint of dashi flavor.

Wasabi

You can add wasabi to the dipping soy sauce or place on the surface of the sushi rice. Some people like wasabi with sushi while others hate it.

Wasabi is made from green wasabi root and offers a strong flavor.

Soy Sauce (Soya Sauce)

Soy sauce is the core sushi ingredients, and sushi is not complete without it.

Sushi grade fish

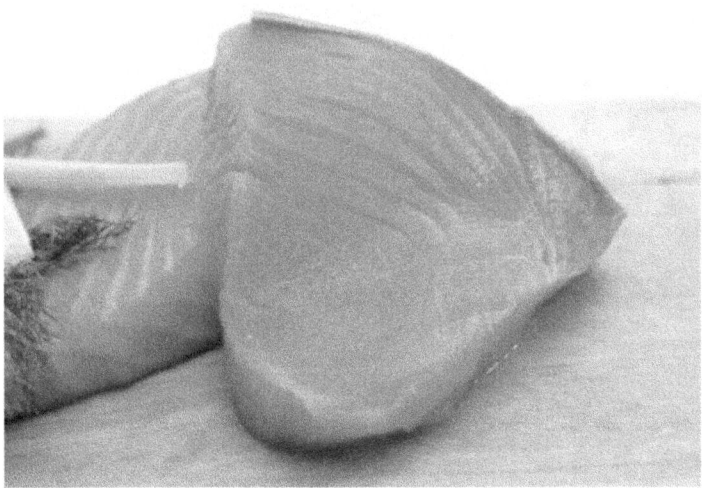

What is sushi grade fish is not clearly defended? You can buy sushi grade fish from the local chain grocery store, order online or from your local Japanese store.

Nori

You need good quality sushi nori to make that perfect sushi. Remember, good quality sushi nori is black and avoid buying any green nori.

Sushi Ginger (Gari)

Gari or sushi ginger is usually served with sushi. Gari is meant to eat between dishes or after sushi to help cleanse the pallet. Enjoy your sushi with gari however you like it.

Green Tea (Ocha)

It is a Japanese tradition that green tea is served with sushi. Like sushi ginger, green tea provides a refreshing break between bites.

Sushi Vegetables

Sushi vegetables such as cucumbers are an important element of sushi. Cucumbers are crisp, clean, refreshing and add balance out the flavors.

DID YOU KNOW?

1) *Japan has the World's Second-Highest Life Expectancy*

Japan is pretty much in a tie with Hong Kong with an average life expectancy of 83.6 years old and 84 years old. Many people attribute Japan's long life expectancy to its traditionally healthier diet when compared to western countries (think more fish and less red meat, more veggies, and smaller portions) how common it is for people to walk as part of their commute, and culture which places extreme importance on family.

2) 69% of Japan is Covered in Forest

When you think of Japan, you probably think of all the different cities there are in the country. Surprisingly the majority of Japan at 69%, is actually covered in forests. I still remember exploring my first forest in Japan in the Mount Fuji area. There was a sign that warned visitors to watch out for black bears and I honestly never thought black bears were roaming the forests in Japan until that moment.

3) Japan has the World's Deepest Underwater Postbox

The deepest underwater postbox is located in Susami, which is a famous fishing town in Wakayama Prefecture and was recorded by Guinness World Records in 2002. The postbox is located 30 feet underwater and since 1999 has collected more than 32,000 pieces of mail.

4) Mount Fuji is a Sacred Place

Mount Fuji isn't just the tallest mountain in Japan, it has also been a sacred place in the Shinto Religion since at least the 7th century. The cool thing is that in the Shinto Religion, the Kami (divine person) of Mount Fuji is Princess Konohanasakuya. Her symbol is the cherry blossom. I was lucky enough to have a chance to visit the Mount Fuji area last year. Although I am not a practitioner of the Shinto Religion, I definitely felt an otherworldly atmosphere and peacefulness as I walked around Lake Kawaguchiko in the shadow of Mount Fuji in the early morning sun.

5) *The Sea of Japan Holds an Abundance of Fish*

The Sea of Japan has a higher than normal concentration of dissolved oxygen which allows many many different species to flourish in the waters. More than 3,500 animal species whichincludes about 1,000 different kinds of fish species call the Sea of Japan their home.

SUSHI SOUP & SALAD RECIPES

1-Healthy Sushi Salad

Time: 54 minutes

Serve: 4

Ingredients:

- 1 cup brown rice;
- 1 avocado, peeled, pitted, and sliced;
- 2 sheet nori, cut into strips;
- 1 cup shelled edamame;
- 1 cucumber, peeled and chopped;
- 2 carrots, chopped;
- 3 green onions, chopped;
- 2 tbsp pickled ginger, chopped;
- 3 tbsp olive oil;
- 1 tbsp sesame seeds;
- ¼ cup sugar;
- ¼ cup rice vinegar;
- 2 ¼ cups water;
- 1 ½ tsp salt; For dressing:
- 2 tbsp soy sauce;
- 3 tbsp water;
- 2 tsp wasabi powder.

Directions:

Add rice and water in a large pot. Bring to simmer; Cover pot with lid and cook on low for 45 minutes; Meanwhile, in a saucepan, add vinegar, salt, and sugar.

Bring to boil and stir until sugar is dissolved. Remove pan from heat;

Transfer cooked rice to a large mixing bowl. Add vinegar mixture and stir well;

Add nori strips, edamame, cucumber, carrot, green onions, ginger, oil, sesame seeds, and remaining vinegar and stir well;

Top with avocado slices;

In a small bowl, mix together all dressing ingredients and drizzle over salad;

Nutritional Value (Amount per Serving):

- **Calories** 532;
- **Fat** 23.9 g;
- **Carbohydrates** 65.4 g;
- **Sugar** 16.8 g;
- **Protein** 10.9 g;
- **Cholesterol** 0 mg.

2-Veggie Sushi Roll Salad

Time: 45 minutes

Serve: 2

Ingredients:

- ¼ cup sushi rice;
- 1 avocado, sliced;
- 4 radishes, sliced;
- 1 carrot, grated;
- 1 romaine lettuce head, chopped;
- 1 tbsp sesame seeds, roasted;

For dressing:

- ¼ tsp ground ginger;
- ½ tsp sesame oil;
- 2 tbsp olive oil;
- 2 tbsp soy sauce;

Directions:

Cook rice according to the packet instructions and set aside to cool.

Take two serving plates and layer the ingredients with lettuce on the bottom, then rice, and veggies. Top with avocado slices.

In a small bowl, whisk togethr all dressing ingredients. Pour dressing over salad and serve.

Nutritional Value (Amount per Serving):

- **Calories** 491;
- **Fat** 37.4 g;
- **Carbohydrates** 37.7 g;
- **Sugar** 4.1 g;
- **Protein** 6.4 g;
- **Cholesterol** 0 mg.

3-Simple Sushi Salad

Time: 15 minutes

Serve: 2

Ingredients:

- 3 cups cooked white rice;
- 1 tbsp sesame seeds;
- 3 nori sheets, cut into small pieces;
- 1 carrot, peeled and diced;
- ½ cucumber, peeled and diced;
- 2 tsp sugar;
- ¼ cup vinegar; 1 tsp sugar.

Directions:

Cook rice according to the packet instructions; Transfer cooked rice into the large mixing bowl;

Add vinegar, sugar, and salt to the rice and toss well;

Add cucumber, carrot, nori sheet, and sesame seeds and toss well;

Nutritional Value (Amount per Serving):

- **Calories** 444;
- **Fat** 2.9 g;
- **Carbohydrates** 93.7 g;
- **Sugar** 8.9 g;
- **Protein** 8.9 g;
- **Cholesterol** 0 mg.

4-Shrimp Sushi Salad

Time: 15 minutes

Serve: 4

Ingredients:

- 2 cups cooked brown rice;
- 1 cup avocado, diced;
- 1 cup cucumber, diced;
- 1 cup carrot, diced;
- ½ lb shrimp, cooked and chopped;
- 1 tbsp chia seeds;
- 2 tbsp vinegar; For dressing:
- 1 tbsp rice vinegar;
- 1 tsp honey;

- 1 tsp sriracha;
- 3 tbsp mayonnaise.

Directions:

In a large bowl, mix together rice, chia seeds, and vinegar; In a small bowl, whisk together all dressing ingredients; Just before serving add cucumber, carrot, and shrimp into the rice and stir well;

Top with avocado and drizzle with dressing; Serve and enjoy.

Nutritional Value (Amount per Serving):

- **Calories** 379;
- **Fat** 13.9 g;
- **Carbohydrates** 47.4 g;
- **Sugar** 4.1 g;
- **Protein** 18.5 g;
- **Cholesterol** 122 mg.

5-Simple Sushi Rice Salad

Time: 25 minutes

Serve: 7

Ingredients:

- 2 cups sushi rice, uncooked;
- 1 tsp sea salt;

- 2 cups water;
- 1 nori sheet, cut into strips;
- 1 tbsp sesame seeds, toasted;
- ¼ cup onion, minced;
- 1 cup cucumber, peeled and chopped; For dressing:
- ¼ tsp prepared wasabi;
- 1 garlic clove, minced;
- 1 tsp ginger, grated;
- 1 tbsp soy sauce;
- 1 tbsp sesame oil;
- 1 tbsp olive oil;
- ½ cup rice vinegar.

Directions:

In a saucepan, add rice, water, and salt. Bring to boil. Cover pan with lid and simmer for 20 minutes;

Remove from heat and uncover and set aside to cool; In a small bowl, mix together all dressing ingredients; Add onion, cucumber, sesame seeds, and dressing to the rice and stir well to combine;

Sprinkle with nori and serve.

Nutritional Value (Amount per Serving):

- **Calories** 253;
- **Fat** 5 g;
- **Carbohydrates** 44 g;
- **Sugar** 0.5 g;
- **Protein** 4.4 g;
- **Cholesterol** 0 mg.

6-Sushi Shiso Salad

Time: 60 minutes

Serve: 8

Ingredients:

- 1 cup brown rice;
- 1 avocado slice;
- 2 green onions, sliced;
- 1 carrot, cut into julienne;
- 1 cucumber, peeled and sliced;
- 1 tbsp pickled ginger, chopped;
- 5 shiso leaves, washed, roll and slice into 1/6 inch pieces;
- 1 nori sheet, cut into strips;
- 1 tbsp avocado oil;
- 1 tbsp honey;
- 2 tbsp mirin;
- 1 tsp wasabi powder;
- 3 tbsp rice vinegar;
- 2 tsp soy sauce;
- 2 cups water;
- ½ tsp sea salt.

Directions:

Add rice, water, and soy sauce to the pot and bring to boil. Reduce heat and cook for 50-55 minutes. Remove from heat and set aside;

In a small bowl, whisk together wasabi powder and vinegar. Mix in honey, oil, mirin, and salt. Pour into the rice and stir gently;

Add shiso leaves and nori to the rice;

Add green onions, carrots, cucumber, and pickled ginger to rice. Mix well and place in refrigerator until chilled;

Top with avocado slice and serve.

Nutritional Value (Amount per Serving):

- **Calories** 135;
- **Fat** 2.5 g;
- **Carbohydrates** 25.2 g;
- **Sugar** 4.3 g;
- **Protein** 2.4 g;
- **Cholesterol** 0 mg.

7- Sushi Salad with Sauce

Time: 60 minutes

Serve: 6

Ingredients:

- 2 cups brown rice;
- 2 tsp fresh lemon juice;
- 2 nori sheets, cut into pieces;
- 1 tbsp sesame seeds;
- 2 avocados, peeled and chopped;
- 2 pears, chopped;
- 1 cucumber, peeled and chopped;
- 4 ½ cups water;

For sauce:

- ¼ tsp red pepper flakes;
- ¼ tsp ground ginger;
- 2 tsp maple syrup;
- 1 tbsp rice vinegar;
- 2 tbsp tamari;
- 1 garlic clove;
- ½ cup peanut butter;
- ½ cup water.

Directions:

For sauce: Add all sauce ingredients into the blender and blend until smooth;

Add rice and water into the saucepan and bring to boil. Reduce heat and simmer for 45-50 minutes. Fluff cooked rice with a fork and set aside;

In a large bowl, mix together lemon juice, avocados, and pears; Add cucumber and sesame seeds and stir well; Add cooked rice, nori, and sauce and stir well; Serve and enjoy.

Nutritional Value (Amount per Serving):

- **Calories** 562;
- **Fat** 26.5 g;
- **Carbohydrates** 73.3 g;
- **Sugar** 11.5 g;
- **Protein** 13.1 g;
- **Cholesterol** 0 mg.

8-Sushi Salmon Salad

Time: 15 minutes

Serve: 4

Ingredients:

- 2 cups cooked brown rice;
- 1 nori sheet, cut into pieces;
- ¼ cup pickled ginger, chopped;
- 1 ¼ cup cucumber, chopped;
- 4 oz smoked salmon, chopped;
- 3 ½ cup arugula;

For dressing:

- ½ tsp sesame oil;
- 2 tsp olive oil;
- ¾ tsp honey;
- 1 tsp wasabi paste;
- 1 tbsp rice vinegar;
- ½ tbsp soy sauce.

Directions:

In a large bowl, add cooked rice, nori, ginger, cucumber, salmon, and arugula and mix well;

In a small bowl, whisk together all sauce ingredients; Pour dressing over salad and stir well;

Serve and enjoy.

Nutritional Value (Amount per Serving):

- **Calories** 444;
- **Fat** 7.5 g;
- **Carbohydrates** 79.8 g;
- **Sugar** 2.3 g;
- **Protein** 14 g;
- **Cholesterol** 7 mg.

9-Sushi Rice Soup

Time: 30 minutes

Serve: 2

Ingredients:

- 2 cups cooked brown rice;
- 10 oz tofu, cut into cubes;
- 1 tbsp tamari;
- 1 tsp sesame seeds;
- 1 tbsp sesame oil;
- 1 tsp miso;
- 1 vegetable stock cube;
- 4 mushrooms, chopped;

- 2 Chinese cabbage leaves, chopped;
- ½ leek, sliced; Pepper; Salt.

Directions:

Add leeks, tamari, sesame seeds, sesame oil, miso, stock cube, mushrooms, cabbage, pepper, and salt in a saucepan with enough water to cover. Bring to boil and cook on low heat until vegetables are cooked;

Add rice and tofu and stir everything well; Stir well and serve.

Nutritional Value (Amount per Serving):

- **Calories** 407;
- **Fat** 15.4 g;
- **Carbohydrates** 52 g;
- **Sugar** 2.8 g;
- **Protein** 19 g;
- **Cholesterol** 0 mg.

10-Miso Soup

Time: 15 minutes

Serve: 2

Ingredients:

- 1 nori sheet, chopped;
- 3 tbsp white miso paste;

- ¼ cup firm tofu, cut into cubed;
- ½ cup green onion, chopped;
- ½ cup green chard, chopped;
- 4 cups water.

Directions:

Add water in a saucepan and simmer over low heat; Add nori and simmer for 5 minutes;

Meanwhile, in a small bowl, add miso and little hot water and whisk until smooth. Set aside;

Add tofu, green onion, and green chard to the saucepan and cook for 5 minutes;

Remove saucepan from heat and add miso mixture and stir well;

Nutritional Value (Amount per Serving):

- **Calories** 88;
- **Fat** 2 g;
- **Carbohydrates** 9 g;
- **Sugar** 2.5 g;
- **Protein** 7 g;
- **Cholesterol** 0 mg.

DID YOU KNOW?

6) Japan is Largely Made Up of 4 Main Islands

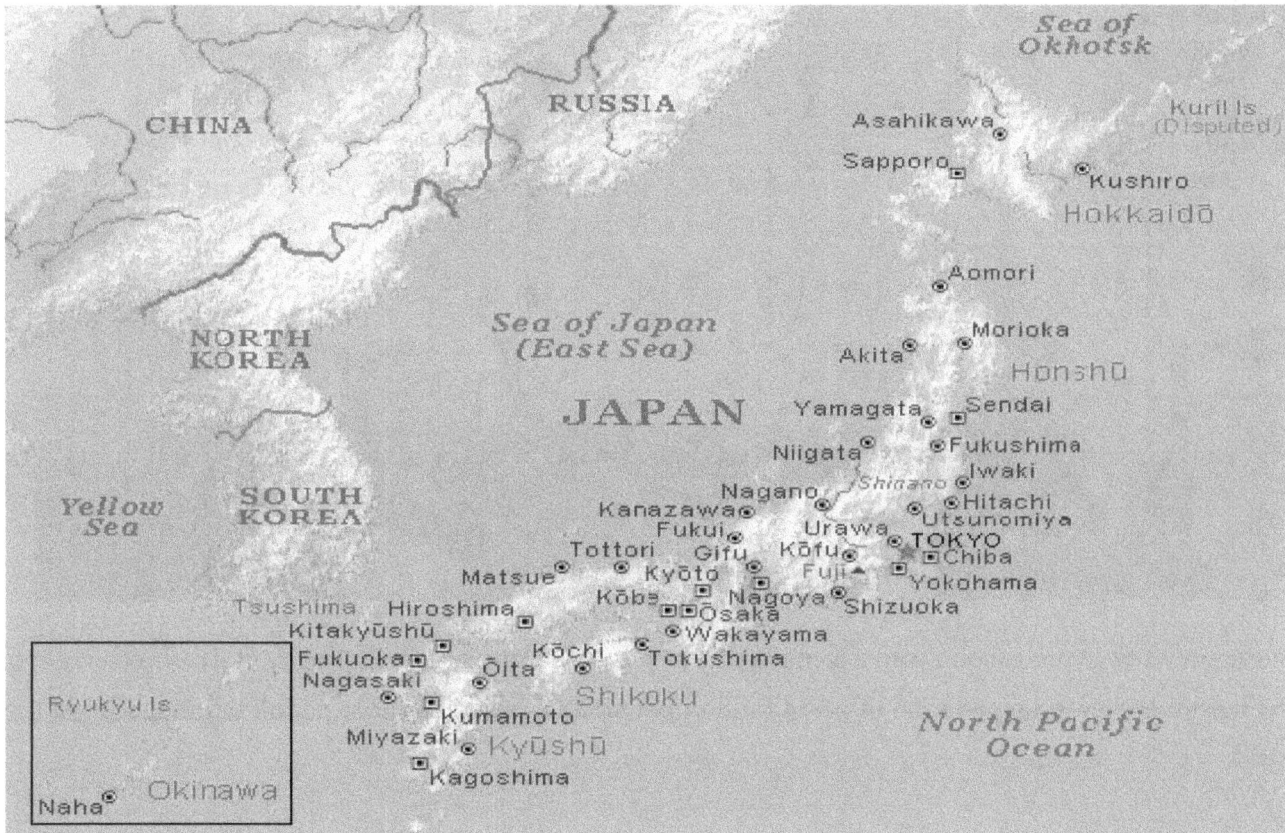

While Japan is an archipelago with almost 6,852 islands, only 4 islands out of all of them make up the majority of Japan's land area. The islands Honshu, Kyushu, Shikoku, and Hokkaido account for 97% of the total area of Japan. The main cities like Tokyo, Osaka, and Kyoto are located on Honshu Island.

7) The Greater Tokyo Area is the Most Populated Megacity in the World

The greater Tokyo metropolitan area is made up of 3 prefectures and includes the capital of Japan, Tokyo, and has an estimated population of 38.14 million people making it the most populated megacity in the world.

VEGETABLE SUSHI RECIPES

11-Avocado Cauliflower Sushi

Time: 20 minutes

Serve: 2

Ingredients:

- 1 cup cauliflower, chopped;
- 1/2 medium avocado;
- 1 tbsp coconut oil;
- 1/4 cup cucumber;
- 1.5 oz cream cheese;
- 1 nori wrapper.

Directions:

Add cauliflower into the food processor and process until it turns into the rice;

Melt coconut oil in the pan over medium-high heat;

Add cauliflower rice into the pan and cook for 5 minutes;

Transfer cauliflower rice into the bowl and set aside;

Slice cucumber, cream cheese, and avocado and set aside; Place long plastic wrap on clean surface;

Place nori wrapper on top of the long plastic wrap; Spread cauliflower rice evenly on nori wrapper;

Layer avocado slices on cauliflower rice on the edges closet to you;

Now layer the cream cheese and cucumber onto avocado; Lift the plastic wrap closet to you;

Using hands cover all the ingredients;

Slowly roll both the wrapper around the ingredients until you have rolled the entire wrapper;

Do not roll plastic wrapper into the sushi; Using knife slice the sushi into pieces; Serve and enjoy.

Nutritional Value (Amount per Serving):

- **Calories** 422;
- **Fat** 24 g;
- **Carbohydrates** 32 g;
- **Sugar** 1 g;
- **Protein** 21 g;
- **Cholesterol** 23 mg.

12-Avocado Peanut Sushi

Time: 35 minutes

Serve: 2

Ingredients:

- 2/3 cup sushi rice;
- 1 tbsp rice vinegar;
- ¾ cup water;
- ¾ tsp salt;
- 2 nori sheets;
- 2 tbsp sesame seeds;
- ½ avocado, sliced into strips;
- 1 tbsp honey;
- 1 tbsp peanut butter;
- ½ cup peanuts, roasted.

Directions:

Add sushi rice, rice vinegar, water, and salt to the saucepan and bring to boil. Reduce heat to low and simmer for 20 minutes. Remove from heat and set aside to cool; Add peanuts, honey, and peanut butter into the food processor and process until all ingredients well mixed;

Place nori sheet on top of the bamboo mat and spread rice evenly on nori. Sprinkle with sesame seeds;

Arrange avocado slice and peanuts mixture on rice layer; Roll nori sheet slowly around the ingredients until you reach to another end of the roll;

Cut roll into the slices and serve.

Nutritional Value (Amount per Serving):

- **Calories** 670;
- **Fat** 36.7 g;
- **Carbohydrates** 71.9 g;
- **Protein** 18.4 g.

13-Avocado Cucumber Sushi

Time: 40 minutes

Serve: 6

Ingredients:

- 1 avocado, peeled and sliced;
- ½ cucumber, sliced into thin strips; 4 nori sheets;
- 3 tbsp rice vinegar; 1 cup sushi rice;
- 1 ½ cups water; 1/8 tsp salt.

Directions:

Add sushi rice, water, vinegar, and salt into the saucepan and bring to boil. Reduce heat to low and simmer for 20 minutes. Remove from heat and set aside to cool;

Place nori sheet on a bamboo mat and spread rice evenly on nori;

Arrange cucumber and avocado slices on rice layer;

Roll nori sheet slowly around the ingredients until you reach to another end of the roll;

Cut roll into the slices and serve.

Nutritional Value (Amount per Serving):

- **Calories** 190;
- **Fat** 6.8 g;
- **Carbohydrates** 28.4 g;
- **Sugar** 0.6 g;
- **Protein** 3 g;
- **Cholesterol** 0 mg.

14-Avocado Cream Cheese Sushi

Time: 30 minutes

Serve: 2

Ingredients:

- ¾ cup sushi rice;
- 1 tbsp onion, diced;
- ½ tsp garlic, minced;
- ½ cup cream cheese;
- ¼ cup cucumber, cut into julienne; 1 avocado, diced;
- 2 nori sheets.

Directions:

Cook sushi rice according to the packet instructions and set aside to cool;

In a small bowl, mix together onion and cream cheese;

Place nori sheet on a bamboo mat and spread cooked sushi rice evenly on nori;

Arrange cucumber and avocado on rice layer. Top with cream cheese mixture;

Roll nori sheet tightly around the ingredients until you reach the other end of the sheet;

Cut roll into the slices and serve.

Nutritional Value (Amount per Serving):

- **Calories** 666;
- **Fat** 40.3 g;
- **Carbohydrates** 66.8 g;
- **Sugar** 1.1 g;
- **Protein** 11.4 g;
- **Cholesterol** 64 mg.

15-Simple Wasabi Cucumber Avocado Sushi

Time: 35 minutes

Serve: 1

Ingredients:

- 1/8 cup sushi rice;

- ½ tsp wasabi;
- 1/8 cup cucumber, sliced into long strips; 1/8 avocado, sliced;
- ½ nori sheet.

Directions:

Cook sushi rice according to the packet instructions;

Place nori sheet on a bamboo mat and spread cooked sushi rice evenly on nori;

Arrange cucumber and avocado on rice layer. Top with wasabi;

Roll nori sheet tightly around the ingredients until you reach the other end of the sheet;

Cut roll into the slices and serve.

Nutritional Value (Amount per Serving):

- **Calories** 139;
- **Fat** 5.1 g;
- **Carbohydrates** 21.4 g;
- **Protein** 2.3 g.

16-Healthy Cucumber Avocado Sushi Roll

Time: 30 minutes

Serve: 4

Ingredients:

- 4 nori sheets;
- 3.5 oz tofu, cut into strips; 1 avocado, sliced;
- 1/2 tbsp sesame seeds, toasted; 1 lb cucumbers, sliced;
- 1 tsp chili powder.

Directions:

Place nori sheet on a clean surface;

Arrange cucumber slices on nori sheet, leaving one-inch margin uncovered;

Sprinkle little chili powder and sesame seeds over cucumber;

Arrange tofu and avocado slices in vertical pattern from the leaf edge;

Roll nori wraps around the ingredients tightly until the nori at the end. Set roll aside for 5 minutes;

Using the same direction make remaining roll;

Take a sharp knife and cut each roll into the pieces and serve.

Nutritional Value (Amount per Serving):

- **Calories** 147;
- **Fat** 11 g;
- **Carbohydrates** 9 g;
- **Sugar** 2 g;
- **Protein** 4 g;
- **Cholesterol** 0 mg.

17-Bell Pepper Avocado Sushi Roll

Time: 30 minutes

Serve: 2

Ingredients:

- 1 bell pepper, chopped; 1/2 avocado, sliced;
- 2 tsp maple syrup; 1/2 tsp tamari;
- 1/2 tsp turmeric;
- 1 cup brown rice, cooked; 2 nori wraps;

Directions:

In a small bowl, combine rice, tamari, maple, and turmeric. Mix well until rice is orange;

Place nori wrap on clean surface and spread half cup rice over 1/3 wrap;

Place on one side few bell pepper and avocado slices;

Tightly roll wrap into the burrito shape with both ends are open;

Cut roll into the slices and serve.

Nutritional Value (Amount per Serving):

- **Calories** 561;
- **Fat** 12 g;
- **Carbohydrates** 96 g;
- **Sugar** 7 g;

- **Protein** 18 g;
- **Cholesterol** 0 mg.

18-Avocado Cucumber Zucchini Sushi Rolls

Time: 15 minutes

Serve: 4

Ingredients:

- 1 avocado, sliced;
- 4 medium radishes, sliced; 1 cucumber, sliced;
- 2 carrots, sliced;
- 3 zucchinis, sliced; 1 tbsp rice vinegar;
- 1/2 cup cashews, soaked overnight.

Directions:

Add soaked cashews and vinegar into the blender and blend until smooth;

Cut both the ends of zucchini and using vegetable peeler peel zucchini into the long strips;

Place zucchini strips on a flat surface;

Spread spoonful cashew paste on one end of zucchini; Arrange few sliced veggies and roll;

Serve and enjoy.

Nutritional Value (Amount per Serving):

- **Calories** 251;
- **Fat** 18 g;
- **Carbohydrates** 20 g;
- **Sugar** 6 g;
- **Protein** 6 g;
- **Cholesterol** 0 mg.

19-Lentil Vegetable Sushi

Time: 55 minutes

Serve: 10

Ingredients:

- 1/3 cup crispy lentils;
- 4 nori seaweed sheets, cut each sheet in half; 1 tbsp rice vinegar;
- 1/2 cup brown rice; 1 1/3 cup water;
- 1/4 scant cup turmeric root, minced; 1 small beet, grated;
- 1 carrot, grated;
- 1/2 cup cilantro, chopped; 1 avocado, sliced;
- 1/4 red cabbage head, sliced.

Directions:

Add water and rice to the pot and bring to boil. Reduce heat and simmer for 45 minutes or until rice sticky;

Stir in rice vinegar;

Place nori sheet on a clean surface;

Spread cooked rice on 1/3 nori sheet evenly;

On top of rice place little avocado, beet, carrot, cabbage, crispy lentils, and turmeric root;

Roll nori sheet around the ingredients until you have rolled the entire sheet;

Using same directions make remaining roll;

Take a sharp knife and cut sushi into pieces and serve.

Nutritional Value (Amount per Serving):

- **Calories** 118;
- **Fat** 4 g;
- **Carbohydrates** 15 g;
- **Sugar** 1 g;
- **Protein** 5 g;
- **Cholesterol** 0 mg.

20-Healthy Veggie Sushi Rolls

Time: 25 minutes

Serve: 1

Ingredients:

- 2 nori sheets;
- 1/2 cup alfalfa sprouts;
- 1/4 zucchini, cut into strips;
- 1/4 large carrot, cut into strips;
- 1/2 bell pepper, cut into strips; 1 avocado, mashed;

For sauce;

- 1 tbsp cilantro, chopped; 1 tbsp lemon juice;
- 1 tsp tamari;
- 1 tbsp Dijon;
- 2 tbsp nutritional yeast; Salt.

Directions:

For sauce: Add all ingredients into the small bowl and mix until well combined;

For sushi roll;

Place nori sheet on clean flat surface; Spread half sauce over nori sheet;

Spread half mashed avocado in evenly on the nori sheet; Arrange slices zucchini, carrots, and bell peppers on top of mashed avocado, parallel to the edges of the wrap;

Place alfalfa sprouts on top;

Slowly roll the nori sheet until reach to another end; Assemble remaining nori sheet using the same method; Cut into slices and serve.

Nutritional Value (Amount per Serving):

- **Calories** 534;
- **Fat** 40 g;
- **Carbohydrate**s 36 g;
- **Sugar** 6 g;
- **Protein** 16 g;
- **Cholesterol** 0 mg.

21-Pear Cucumber Sushi

Time: 55 minutes

Serve: 4

Ingredients:

- 4 nori sheets;
- 1/4 cucumber, sliced; 1/2 avocado, sliced; 1 pear, sliced;
- 1 tbsp maple syrup;
- 1 tbsp brown rice vinegar; 2 cups water;
- 1 cup brown rice, uncooked.

Directions:

Add water and rice to the pot and bring to boil. Reduce heat and simmer for 45 minutes;

Transfer cooked rice into the bowl;

Add maple syrup and vinegar into the cooked rice mix well; Place nori sheet on the clean and plain surface; Spread cooked brown rice evenly on the nori sheet; Arrange sliced cucumber, avocado, and pear on rice layer; Roll nori sheet around the ingredients tightly until you reach the other end;

Set prepare sushi roll aside for 5 minutes;

Using a sharp knife cut the roll into the slices and serve.

Nutritional Value (Amount per Serving):

- **Calories** 264;
- **Fat** 6 g;
- **Carbohydrates** 48 g;
- **Sugar** 6 g;
- **Protein** 4 g;
- **Cholesterol** 0 mg.

22-Healthy Vegetarian Sushi

Time: 30 minutes

Serve: 4

Ingredients:

- 1 cup sushi rice; 1 1/2 cup water;
- 1/4 cup spinach, sliced; 1 carrot, sliced;

- 1 zucchini, sliced; 1/2 avocado, sliced;
- 1/2 bell pepper, sliced; 4 nori sheets;
- 1 tsp sugar;
- 3 tbsp rice vinegar; 1 tsp salt.

Directions:

Add water and rice to the pot and bring to boil. Reduce heat and simmer for 10 minutes;

Transfer cooked rice into the bowl;

Add sugar, vinegar, and salt into the rice and mix well; Place nori sheet on a flat surface and spread cooked rice evenly on the nori sheet;

Lay slices of carrots, zucchini, avocado, bell pepper, and spinach on top of rice;

Moisten both the ends of the nori sheet with water;

Roll the nori wrap around the ingredients tightly until you reach the other end;

Let sit sushi roll for few minutes then using sharp knife cut into the slices and serve.

Nutritional Value (Amount per Serving):

- **Calories** 253;
- **Fat** 5.4 g;
- **Carbohydrates** 44 g;
- **Sugar** 3 g;
- **Protein** 5 g;
- **Cholesterol** 0 mg.

23-Vegetable Quinoa Sushi Rolls

Time: 30 minutes

Serve: 4

Ingredients:

- 4 nori sheets;
- 1/2 cucumber, sliced; 1/2 avocado, sliced; 2 cups water;
- 1 cup quinoa, rinse and drained; 100g spinach.

Directions:

Add quinoa and water to the pot. Cover pot and cook for 15 minutes;

Remove cooked quinoa into the large bowl and set aside to cool;

Place nori sheet on the clean and plain surface;

Spread cooked quinoa evenly on the nori sheet;

Arrange sliced cucumber, spinach, and avocado on top of quinoa layer;

Slowly roll the nori sheet until you reach to another end; Cut roll into the slices and serve.

Nutritional Value (Amount per Serving):

- **Calories** 221;
- **Fat** 7 g;
- **Carbohydrates** 32 g;
- **Sugar** 0.9 g;

- **Protein** 7 g;
- **Cholesterol** 0 mg.

24-Asian Sushi Rolls

Time: 30 minutes

Serve: 24

Ingredients:

- 1 avocado, cut into strips; 1 carrot, shredded;
- 1 bell pepper, cut into strips; 1 cucumber, cut into strips; 1 tbsp mirin;
- 3 tbsp sugar;
- 3 tbsp rice vinegar; 2 1/4 cups water;
- 2 cups rice, medium grain; 2 tsp salt;
- Nori sheets.

Directions:

Wash rice well and add water and rice into the steamer and cooked according to the steamer instruction;

Transfer cooked rice into the bowl;

Add sugar, vinegar, and salt into the rice and mix well; Place nori sheet on the plain and clean surface; Spread cooked rice evenly on the nori sheet;

Layer sliced veggies over the rice; Roll slowly nori sheet around the ingredients until reach the other end;

Cut roll into the slices and serve.

Nutritional Value (Amount per Serving):

- **Calories** 86;
- **Fat** 1 g;
- **Carbohydrates** 15 g;
- **Sugar** 2 g;
- **Protein** 1 g;
- **Cholesterol** 0 mg.

25-Veggie Cream Cheese Sushi

Time: 30 minutes

Serve: 2

Ingredients:

- 2/3 cup sushi rice;
- 1 tbsp rice vinegar;
- ¾ cup water;
- ¾ tsp salt;
- 2 nori sheets;
- ¼ cup cream cheese; 2 scallions, chopped;
- ½ cucumber, sliced into matchstick strips;
- 4 asparagus spears, trimmed.

Directions:

Add rice, vinegar, water, and salt in a saucepan and bring to boil. Reduce heat to low and simmer for 20 minutes; Remove from heat and set aside to cool;

Place nori sheet on a bamboo mat and spread cooked rice on nori sheet evenly;

Arrange cucumber, asparagus, scallions, and cream cheese on rice layer;

Roll nori sheet slowly around the ingredients until you reach to another end of the roll;

Cut roll into the slices and serve.

Nutritional Value (Amount per Serving):

- **Calories** 357;
- **Fat** 10.7 g;
- **Carbohydrates** 55.8 g;
- **Protein** 8.4 g.

26-Sweet Potato Sushi

Time: 40 minutes

Serve: 3

Ingredients:

- 1 lb sweet potato, peel and cut into fries shape;
- 1 tsp sesame oil;

- 1 tbsp maple syrup; 1 tbsp olive oil;
- 1 cup sushi rice;
- 1 ½ tbsp rice vinegar; 1 1/3 cups water;
- ¾ tsp salt;
- 3 nori sheets.

Directions:

Preheat the oven to 375 F;

Spray a baking tray with cooking spray;

In a small bowl, mix together olive oil, sesame oil, and maple syrup;

Add sweet potato fries in a bowl. Pour olive oil mixture and toss well;

Arrange potato fries on a baking tray and bake for 25 minutes. Turn halfway through;

Meanwhile, Add rice, water, vinegar, and salt in a saucepan and heat over high heat. Reduce heat and simmer for 20 minutes. Remove from heat and set aside to cool;

Place nori sheet on a bamboo mat and spread sushi rice on nori evenly;

Arrange sweet potato fries on the rice layer;

Roll nori sheet slowly around the ingredients until you reach to another end of the roll;

Cut roll into the slices and serve.

Nutritional Value (Amount per Serving):

- **Calories** 437;
- **Fat** 6.9 g;
- **Carbohydrates** 85.1 g;
- **Protein** 7.5 g;
- **Cholesterol** 0 mg.

27-Miso Carrot Sushi

Time: 40 minutes

Serve: 12

Ingredients:

For rice:

- 3/4 cup sushi rice;
- 1 tbsp sesame seeds, toasted; 2 nori sheets;
- 1 tsp sugar;
- ½ tbsp mirin;
- 1 tbsp rice vinegar; 1 cup water;

For carrots:

- 1 large carrot, peeled and sliced into matchstick size;
- ¼ tsp paprika;
- 1 tsp maple syrup;
- 2 tsp soy sauce;
- 2 tsp balsamic vinegar; 2 tsp miso paste;
- ½ tsp ginger, grated;
- ½ tsp olive oil.

Directions:

Preheat the oven to 400 F;

Toss carrots with olive oil and place in baking tray; Roast carrot in preheated oven for 10 minutes;

In a small bowl, whisk together paprika, maple syrup, soy sauce, balsamic vinegar, miso paste, and ginger;

Pour paprika mixture over carrots and mix well;

Return carrots in the oven and roast for 10 minutes more. Transfer carrots to the place and set aside to cool;

Add rice, mirin, sugar, rice vinegar, and water in a saucepan and bring to boil over medium heat. Remove rice from heat and set aside to cool;

Place nori sheet on a bamboo mat and spread cook sushi rice evenly on nori;

Sprinkle toasted sesame seeds over rice; Arrange roasted carrots on the rice layer;

Roll nori sheet tightly around the ingredients until you reach the other end of the sheet;

Cut roll into the slices and serve.

Nutritional Value (Amount per Serving):

- **Calories** 58;
- **Fat** 0.7 g;
- **Carbohydrates** 11.4 g;
- **Protein** 1.2 g.

28-Cucumber Mango Sushi

Time: 15 minutes

Serve: 2

Ingredients:

- 1 cucumber, sliced;
- 1 cup cooked sushi rice;
- ½ fresh mango, sliced;
- 1 avocado, sliced;
- 2 nori sheets;
- 1 tbsp sesame seeds, toasted.

Directions:

Place nori sheet on a bamboo mat and spread cooked sushi rice evenly on rice layer;

Sprinkle sesame seeds on rice then arrange cucumber, mango, and avocado on rice layer;

Roll nori sheet tightly around the ingredients until you reach the other end of the sheet;

Cut roll into the slices and serve.

Nutritional Value (Amount per Serving):

- **Calories** 641;
- **Fat** 22.9 g;
- **Carbohydrates** 101.7 g;
- **Protein** 11 g.

29-Mix Vegetable Sushi

Time: 35 minutes

Serve: 3

Ingredients:

- 1 1/8 cup sushi rice; 3 nori sheets;
- ½ beetroot, sliced into strips;
- ½ cucumber, sliced into strips;
- ¼ yellow bell pepper, sliced into strips;
- ½ carrot, sliced into strips; 3 tbsp rice vinegar.

Directions

Cook sushi rice according to the packet instruction. Remove from heat and set aside to cool. Add vinegar into the cooked rice and stir well;

Place nori sheet on a bamboo mat and spread rice evenly on nori;

Arrange all the vegetables on the rice layer;

Roll nori sheet tightly around the ingredients until you reach the other end of the sheet; Cut roll into the slices and serve.

Nutritional Value (Amount per Serving):

- **Calories** 278;
- **Fat** 0.5 g;
- **Carbohydrates** 59 g;
- **Sugar** 1.9 g;
- **Protein** 5.5 g;
- **Cholesterol** 0 mg.

DID YOU KNOW?

8) The Portuguese were the First Europeans to Visit Japan

The first Europeans to visit Japan were the Portuguese in the year 1543 when they landed at the Port of Nagasaki. This first visit from the Portuguese marked the beginning of the Nanban trade period which lasted from 1543 to 1614.

During this period, the Japanese and Portuguese freely traded goods with each other, and new technologies and cultural practices such as European guns, European armor, and European ships were introduced to Japan.

Another surprising fact from this period is that the Portuguese actually introduced tempura to Japan, which is now one of the most popular dishes in all of Japan.

9) Japan had a Period of Complete Isolation from the Rest of the World

Because of the massive influence that European culture was having on Japan, since first meeting them in 1543, the Shogun of Japan at that time Tokugawa Iemitsu closed off Japan to all foreigners in 1635. During this time, anyone who was seen using European goods would be punished. This law was called the Sakoku Edict of 1635 and lasted over 200 years.

10) Japan has a Word for Death by Overwork, "Karoshi"

One of the first things you'll notice when you visit Japan is just how hard everyone works, especially the Salarymen and Salarywomen in the big cities of Japan. Every day during morning rush hour, you'll see men and women in dark-colored suits sardine themselves onto the subway in order to get to work on time.

11) One Heck of a Healthy Diet

The Japanese diet is definitely known throughout the world as being one of the healthiest diets. With traditional diets staples that include plenty of rice, fish, and vegetables, people in Japan tend to eat less fatty foods richer in vitamins and minerals. Their diet is one of the factors to the long life expectancy in Japan.

Meat and Egg Sushi Recipes

30-Delicious Chicken Sushi

Time: 30 minutes

Serve: 24

Ingredients:

- 1 cup sushi rice;
- 1/2 cup blue cheese, crumbled; 2 carrots, cut into strips;
- 2 celery ribs, cut into strips; 1/4 cup hot sauce;
- 1 cup chicken, cooked and shredded; 4 nori sheets;
- 1 tbsp sugar;
- 1/4 cup rice wine vinegar; 2 cups water;
- 1/2 tsp salt;

Directions:

Add water and rice to the pot and bring to boil; Reduce heat and simmer for 20 minutes;

Meanwhile, in a pan heat sugar, vinegar, and salt until sugar is dissolved. Remove from heat and set aside to cool; Transfer cooked rice into the large bowl;

Add sugar mixture to the rice and mix well; Place nori sheet on the clean and plain surface; Spread cooked rice evenly on 3/4 nori sheet;

Place chicken, carrots, celery, and blue cheese on top of rice;

Slowly roll nori sheet until you reach to another end; Cut roll into the slices and serve.

Nutritional Value (Amount per Serving):

- **Calories** 54;
- **Fat** 1 g;
- **Carbohydrates** 7 g;
- **Sugar** 0.8 g;
- **Protein** 3 g;
- **Cholesterol** 7 mg.

31-Spicy Chicken Sushi

Time: 30 minutes

Serve: 4

Ingredients:

- 1 cup chicken, shredded; 1 tbsp sriracha sauce;
- 3 1/2 tbsp mayo; 2 nori sheets;
- 1 large avocado, sliced; 1 cucumber, sliced;
- 1 1/2 cups sushi rice, cooked.

Directions:

In a mixing bowl, mix together chicken, sriracha, and mayo and set aside;

Place nori sheet on the clean and plain surface; Spread warm rice evenly on the nori sheet;

Arrange slices avocado and cucumber on rice layer;

Roll nori wrap tightly around ingredients until you reach the other end;

Slice sushi roll using a sharp knife and serve.

Nutritional Value (Amount per Serving):

- **Calories** 470;
- **Fat** 15 g;
- **Carbohydrates** 65 g;
- **Sugar** 2 g;
- **Protein** 16 g;
- **Cholesterol** 30 mg.

32-Fried Chicken Sushi Rolls

Time: 25 minutes

Serve: 2

Ingredients:

- 1 chicken breast, fried and cut into pieces;
- 3 lettuce leaves;
- 1 tbsp sugar;
- 2 tbsp vinegar;
- 2 cups rice, cooked;
- 2 nori sheets;
- 1/2 tsp salt.

Directions:

Place cooked rice into the bowl;

Add vinegar, sugar, and salt into the rice and mix well; Place nori sheet on the clean and plain surface; Spread rice evenly on the nori sheet;

Place lettuce leaves on rice layer;

Add chicken on lettuce and roll nori sheet tightly around the ingredients until you reach to another end;

Cut roll into the slices and serve.

Nutritional Value (Amount per Serving):

- **Calories** 761;
- **Fat** 2 g;
- **Carbohydrates** 154 g;
- **Sugar** 6 g;
- **Protein** 24 g;
- **Cholesterol** 32 mg.

33-Teriyaki Beef Sushi

Time: 40 minutes

Serve: 4

Ingredients:

- 13 oz beef fillet, sliced;

- 1 tbsp chives, chopped;
- 1 tbsp lemon juice;
- 2 tsp fresh ginger, grated;
- 2 cups brown rice, cooked;
- 4 nori sheets;
- 1 medium carrot, sliced;
- 8 green shallots, ends trimmed;
- 1/4 cup teriyaki sauce.

Directions:

In a bowl, add beef slices and teriyaki sauce and set aside for 30 minutes;

Heat grill over high heat;

Spray grill using cooking spray;

Place carrots and shallot on hot grill and grill for 2 minutes. Remove from grill and set aside;

Place nori sheet on a clean surface;

Spread cooked rice evenly on nori sheet then place beef slices, carrots, and shallots;

Roll nori sheet tightly around the ingredients until you reach to another end;

Using the same direction make remaining roll; Cut roll into the slices and serve.

Nutritional Value (Amount per Serving):

- **Calories** 544;
- **Fat** 8 g;
- **Carbohydrates** 77 g;
- **Sugar** 3 g;
- **Protein** 36 g;
- **Cholesterol** 82 mg.

34-Sweet and Spicy Chicken Sushi

Time: 40 minutes

Serve: 24

Ingredients:

- 1 cup sushi rice;
- 2 tbsp mayonnaise;
- 4 nori sheets;
- 1/4 cup mirin seasoning;
- 4 chicken tenderloins, cut into strips and cooked; 1/4 cup sweet chili sauce;
- 1/2 medium avocado, sliced; 1/2 cucumber, cut into strips; 4 lettuce leaves, torn.

Directions:

Add rice and 1 cup water into the saucepan and bring to boil;

Reduce heat and simmer for 12 minutes; Transfer cooked rice into the large bowl;

Add mirin seasoning and sweet chili sauce into the rice and mix well;

Place nori sheet on the clean and plain surface; Spread cooked rice evenly on the nori sheet; Spread mayonnaise on the rice layer;

Place lettuce leaves, avocado, cucumber and chicken and roll the nori sheet tightly around the ingredients until you reach to another end;

Using a sharp knife cut the roll into the slices and serve.

Nutritional Value (Amount per Serving):

- **Calories** 270;
- **Fat** 3 g;
- **Carbohydrates** 5 g;
- **Protein** 3 g;
- **Cholesterol** 11 mg.

35-Yummy Chicken Schnitzel Sushi Rolls

Time: 40 minutes

Serve: 6

Ingredients:

- 2 1/2 cups sushi rice; 2 1/2 cups water;
- 6 nori sheets;
- 1/4 cup mayonnaise;
- 1/4 cup sushi seasoning; 2 tbsp olive oil;
- 11 oz chicken schnitzels, crumbled; 1 avocado, sliced.

Directions:

Add water and rice to the saucepan and bring to boil. Reduce heat and simmer for 10 minutes;

Transfer cooked rice into the large bowl;

Add sushi seasoning into the rice and mix well; Heat olive oil in a pan over medium heat;

Add chicken to the pan and cook for 4 minutes on each side; Cut chicken into the pieces;

Place nori sheet on clean and plane surface; Spread cooked rice evenly on the nori sheet; Spread mayonnaise on the rice layer;

Place avocado and chicken slices and roll nori sheet tightly until you reach the other end;

Cut roll into the slices and serve.

Nutritional Value (Amount per Serving):

- **Calories** 797;
- **Fat** 22 g;
- **Carbohydrates** 95 g;
- **Sugar** 2 g;
- **Protein** 54 g;
- **Cholesterol** 3 mg.

36-Brown Rice Chicken Sushi Rolls

Time: 40 minutes

Serve: 8

Ingredients:

- 1 cup brown rice;
- 1 tbsp rice vinegar;
- 2 tsp sesame oil;
- 1 tsp honey;

- 1/2 tsp chili sauce;
- 4 nori sheets;
- 1 cucumber, cut in strips;
- 1/2 avocado, pitted and sliced;
- 1 chicken breast, boneless and skinless;
- 1/2 tsp olive oil;
- 1/4 cup mayonnaise;
- 2 tsp tamari;

Directions:

Cook brown rice according to the packet instruction; Transfer cooked rice into the large bowl and add rice vinegar to the rice and mix well;

Heat olive oil in a pan over medium heat;

Add chicken to the pan and cook for 12 minutes or until golden brown;

Cut cooked chicken into the pieces;

In a small bowl, mix together sesame oil, honey, chili sauce, mayonnaise, and tamari;

Place nori sheet on the clean and plain surface; Spread cooked brown rice evenly on the nori sheet; Spread sesame oil mixture on rice layer;

Arrange chicken, cucumber and avocado slices and roll the nori sheet tightly around the ingredients until you reach to another end;

Cut roll into the slices and serve.

Nutritional Value (Amount per Serving):

- **Calories** 178;
- **Fat** 7 g;
- **Carbohydrates** 23 g;
- **Protein** 5 g;
- **Cholesterol** 10 mg.

37-Egg Chicken Sushi Rolls

Time: 30 minutes

Serve: 4

Ingredients:

- 6 eggs;
- 4 nori sheets;
- 2 chicken thighs, cooked and shredded; 2 tbsp mayonnaise;
- 1 tbsp coriander, chopped; 2 tbsp coconut oil;
- 1/4 tsp sea salt;
- small carrots, sliced; 1 avocados, sliced.

Directions:

In a bowl, whisk together egg, salt, and coriander; Heat pan over medium-high heat;

Add 1 tsp of coconut oil in a pan. Once the oil is hot then add 5 tbsp egg mixture to the pan and cook until omelet is golden brown;

Repeat same with remaining egg mixture; Place nori sheet on the clean and plain surface; Place one omelet on the nori sheet;

Spread 1 tsp of mayonnaise on omelet then arrange carrot, avocado, and chicken;

Roll nori sheet tightly around the ingredients until you reach to another end;

Cut roll into the slices and serve.

Nutritional Value (Amount per Serving):

- **Calories** 430;
- **Fat** 31 g;
- **Carbohydrates** 8 g;
- **Sugar** 1 g;
- **Protein** 31 g;
- **Cholesterol** 312 mg.

38-Veggie Chicken Sushi Rolls

Time: 30 minutes

Serve: 4

Ingredients:

- 2 cups sushi rice;
- 1 packet nori sheet;
- 1.3 lbs chicken schnitzels;
- 100 ml sushi seasoning;
- 1 red bell pepper;
- 1 avocado; 1/2 cucumber;
- 1 carrot.

Directions:

Add rice and water to the pot and bring to boil. Reduce heat and simmer for 20 minutes;

Spray pan with cooking spray and heat over medium heat;

Add chicken in pan and cook for 4 minutes on each side; Remove cooked chicken from pan and cut into pieces; Place nori sheet on clean and plane surface and spread rice evenly on the nori sheet;

Arrange vegetables and chicken on rice layer;

Slowly roll the nori sheet until you reach to another end; Cut roll into the slices and serve.

Nutritional Value (Amount per Serving):

- **Calories** 1027;
- **Fat** 11 g;
- **Carbohydrates** 213 g;
- **Sugar** 103 g;
- **Protein** 16 g;
- **Cholesterol** 0 mg.

39-Ham Egg Sushi

Time: 55 minutes

Serve: 4

Ingredients:

- 1/4 cup rice vinegar;
- 2 cups water;
- 2 cups sushi rice;

- 1 tsp olive oil;
- 2 eggs, beaten;
- 1/2 cup spinach, chopped; 1/4 tsp salt;
- 6 ham slices, cooked; 4 nori sheets;

Directions:

Add rice and water to the pot and bring to boil. Reduce heat and simmer for 20 minutes;

Transfer cooked rice into the large bowl;

Add rice vinegar to the rice and mix well; Heat olive oil in a pan over medium heat;

In a bowl, whisk together egg, spinach, and salt;

Add egg mixture to the pan and cook until egg is fully cooked;

Remove pan from heat and set aside to cool; Place nori sheet on the clean and plain surface; Spread cooked rice evenly on the nori sheet;

Place ham slices on rice layer then place egg mixture;

Roll nori sheet tightly around the ingredients until you reach to another end;

Using a sharp knife cut the roll into the slices and serve.

Nutritional Value (Amount per Serving):

- **Calories** 480;
- **Fat** 6 g;
- **Carbohydrates** 86 g;
- **Protein** 19 g;
- **Cholesterol** 175 mg.

40-Egg Omelet Nigiri

Time: 20 minutes

Serve: 10

Ingredients:

- 4 eggs;
- 1 tsp olive oil;
- 2 cups sushi rice;
- Pepper;
- Salt.

Directions:

Heat oil in a pan over medium heat; Whisk egg, pepper, and salt together. Once the oil is hot then pour egg mixture into the pan and spread well and cook until eggs are set;

Flip omelet on a plate and slice into a rectangle shape;

Divide sushi rice into 10 equal portions and shape each portion into a rectangle with moistened hands;

Place omelet slices on top of rice; Serve and enjoy.

Nutritional Value (Amount per Serving):

Calories 164;

Fat 2.5 g;

Carbohydrates 29.7 g;

Protein 4.9 g.

41-Pesto Egg Sushi

Time: 25 minutes

Serve: 36

Ingredients:

- 6 eggs, lightly beaten;
- ¼ cup basil pesto;
- 6 nori sheets;
- 4 cups water;
- 2 cups sushi rice;
- Pepper;
- Salt.

Directions:

Add rice and water to the saucepan and bring to boil. Turn heat to low and simmer for 20 minutes. Remove from heat and set aside to cool;

Spray pan with cooking spray and heat over medium heat;

Add eggs to the pan and scramble until cooked through. Season with pepper and salt;

Remove scrambled egg from heat and set aside;

Place nori sheet on bamboo mat. Spread cooked sushi rice evenly on the nori sheet;

Spread pesto on rice then top with scrambled egg; Slowly roll the nori sheet around the ingredients until you reach the other end of the roll;

Cut roll into the slices and serve.

Nutritional Value (Amount per Serving):

- **Calories** 48;
- **Fat** 0.8 g;
- **Carbohydrates** 8.3 g;
- **Protein** 1.7 g;
- **Cholesterol** 27 mg.

42-Edamame Egg Sushi

Time: 25 minutes

Serve: 8

Ingredients:

- 4 cups cooked sushi rice; 2 tbsp sugar;
- 2 tbsp rice vinegar; 4 nori sheets;
- 4 eggs;
- ½ cup edamame;
- 1 tbsp olive oil;
- Pepper;
- Salt.

Directions:

Transfer cooked rice in a bowl, Add sugar and rice to the rice and mix well;

Heat oil in a pan over medium heat;

Whisk eggs with pepper and salt and pour into the hot pan. Spread egg evenly and cook until eggs are set;

Flip omelet on a plate and cut into strips; Place nori sheet on bamboo mat;

Spread cooked rice evenly on the nori sheet; Place egg strip and edamame on rice;

Slowly roll the nori sheet around the ingredients until you reach the other end of the roll;

Cut roll into the slices and serve.

Nutritional Value (Amount per Serving):

- **Calories** 114;
- **Fat** 5.1 g;
- **Carbohydrates** 11.6 g;
- **Sugar** 3.2 g;
- **Protein** 5.4 g;
- **Cholesterol** 82 mg.

43-Egg Avocado Sushi Rolls

Time: 25 minutes

Serve: 8

Ingredients:

- 4 cups cooked sushi rice;
- 2 scrambled eggs;
- 1 avocado, sliced;
- ½ tbsp vinegar;
- 4 nori sheets;
- ¼ cup mayonnaise; Salt.

Directions:

Transfer cooked sushi rice in a mixing bowl. Add sugar, vinegar, and salt to the rice and mix well;

Place nori sheet on bamboo mat. Spread rice evenly on the nori sheet;

Arrange scrambled egg and avocado on rice. Top with mayonnaise;

Slowly roll the nori sheet around the ingredients until you reach the other end of the roll;

Cut roll into the slices and serve.

Nutritional Value (Amount per Serving):

- **Calories** 217;
- **Fat** 8.6 g;
- **Carbohydrates** 30.7 g;

- **Sugar** 0.7 g;
- **Protein** 4.1 g;
- **Cholesterol** 43 mg.

44-Egg Smoked Salmon Sushi Rolls

Time: 40 minutes

Serve: 6

Ingredients:

- 2 scrambled eggs;
- 6 nori sheets;
- 6 tbsp rice wine vinegar; 2 cups sushi rice;
- 8 oz smoked salmon, cut into strips; 1 cucumber, sliced;
- 1 avocado, sliced.

Directions:

Cook sushi rice according to the packet instructions;

Once rice is cool then add vinegar to the rice and mix well; Place nori sheet on a bamboo mat and spread rice evenly on the nori sheet;

Place salmon, cucumber, avocado, and scrambled egg on rice layer;

Roll nori sheet slowly around the ingredients until you reach to another end of the roll;

Cut roll into the slices and serve.

Nutritional Value (Amount per Serving):

- **Calories** 376;
- **Fat** 10.1 g;
- **Carbohydrates** 54.1 g;
- **Sugar** 1.2 g;
- **Protein** 14.1 g;
- **Cholesterol** 63 mg.

DID YOU KNOW?

12) A Banned Pokemon Episode

On December 16, 1997, an episode of Pokemon aired in Japan that actually caused 700 children to have medical issues and had to be sent to the hospital. At the most end, some of the kids even had seizures. The reason for so many kids being affected by this episode was the strobe lighting. Plus, at the time, Pokemon was one of the most popular shows in Japan, so many kids were watching the episode which increased the odds of people being affected.

13) The Political Structure of Japan

Because of the country's size, the country has been politically structured into 8 different regions and 47 different prefectures. The prefectures actually go back to the Meiji Period (1868 – 1912), which were created to replace the lands controlled by the Daimyo, the powerful feudal lords who ruled the country before the Meiji Period.

14) Japan is a Country of Varying Climates

Since Japan geographically stretches from North to South for such a long distance, the climate in different areas of the country tends to vary by a good amount. The climate in some of the big cities like Tokyo ranges from a temperate to subtropical climate. This means hot summers and mild winters, and 4 different seasons.

On the other hand, the climate across the northern island of Hokkaido is much cooler. The summers are nice and mild, but in the winter the area gets a ton of snow and the temperature often drops below freezing.

Tofu Sushi Recipes

45-Spicy Vegetable Tofu Sushi Rolls

Time: 30 minutes

Serve: 2

Ingredients:

- 1/2 avocado, cut into slices; 1 tsp garlic powder;
- 1/2 pack firm tofu;
- 1/2 tbsp sesame seeds; 2 tsp sriracha sauce;
- 1 tbsp mayo;
- 2 nori sheets;
- 1 tbsp sugar;
- 1/3 cup rice vinegar;
- 1 cup sushi rice, cooked.

Directions:

Add warm cooked rice into the mixing bowl; Add sugar and vinegar to the rice and mix well;

Squeeze out excess liquid from tofu and crumble the tofu; Add garlic powder, sriracha, and mayo into the tofu and mix well;

Place nori sheet on clean and plane surface and spread rice evenly on the nori sheet;

Spread tofu mixture on rice layer and arrange some avocado slices;

Slowly roll nori sheet around the ingredients tightly until you reach to another end;

Cut roll into the slices and serve.

Nutritional Value (Amount per Serving):

- **Calories** 585;
- **Fat** 18.2 g;
- **Carbohydrates** 88 g;
- **Sugar** 7 g;
- **Protein** 10 g;
- **Cholesterol** 5 mg.

46-Tofu Sushi Rolls

Time: 15 minutes

Serve: 3

Ingredients:

- 1 cup cooked sushi rice; 1 tbsp sugar;
- 1/3 cup rice vinegar; 3 nori sheets;
- ½ avocado, peeled and cut into slice; 1 tsp garlic powder;
- ½ package firm tofu;
- ½ tbsp sesame seeds; 2 tsp sriracha;

- 1 tbsp mayonnaise.

Directions:

Transfer cooked sushi rice in a large bowl. Add rice vinegar, and sugar to the rice and mix well;

In another bowl, add tofu and crumble it. Add mayo, sriracha, sesame seeds, and garlic powder to the crumbled tofu and mix well;

Place nori sheet on a bamboo mat and spread cooked sushi rice on nori;

Arrange avocado slice and tofu mixture on rice layer;

Roll nori sheet slowly around the ingredients until you reach to another end of the roll;

Cut roll into the slices and serve.

Nutritional Value (Amount per Serving):

- **Calories** 360;
- **Fat** 9.3 g;
- **Carbohydrates** 59.1 g;
- **Protein** 5.5 g.

47- Vegetable Tofu Sushi

Time: 55 minutes

Serve: 6

Ingredients:

- 6 nori sheets;
- 1 cucumber, sliced;
- 6 green onion, chopped;
- 1 1/2 medium avocados, sliced;
- 2 carrots, cut into strips;
- 1 lb firm tofu, drained;
- 4 1/2 cups sushi rice, cooked.

Directions:

Cut tofu into the slices;

Place nori sheet on clean and plane surface; Spread cooked sushi rice evenly on the nori sheet;

Arrange cucumber, green onion, avocado, carrot, and tofu on rice layer;

Roll nori sheet tightly around the ingredients until you reach to another end;

Using a sharp knife cut the roll into the slices and serve.

Nutritional Value (Amount per Serving):

- **Calories** 685;
- **Fat** 14 g;
- **Carbohydrates** 121 g;
- **Sugar** 3 g;
- **Protein** 18 g;
- **Cholesterol** 0 mg.

48-Spicy Tofu Sushi

Time: 50 minutes

Serve: 4

Ingredients:

- 1 cup sushi rice, cooked and seasoned; 2 nori sheets;
- 1 tbsp sesame seed; 1 green onion, sliced;
- 1 1/2 tbsp mayonnaise;
- 4 oz firm tofu, cut into cubes; 1/4 tsp hot chili oil;

Directions:

Spray pan with cooking spray and heat over medium heat; Add tofu to the pan and cook until golden brown on all the sides;

Transfer tofu into the mixing bowl;

Add sesame seed, green onion, mayonnaise, and chili oil into the tofu and mash tofu well;

Place nori sheet on the plain surface then spread cooked rice evenly on the nori sheet;

Place tofu mixture and green onion on rice layer;

Roll nori sheet slowly around the ingredients until you reach to another end of the roll;

Cut roll into the slices and serve.

Nutritional Value (Amount per Serving):

- **Calories** 228;
- **Fat** 4 g;
- **Carbohydrates** 39 g;
- **Sugar** 0.7 g;
- **Protein** 6 g;
- **Cholesterol** 1 mg.

49- Smoky Tofu Sushi

Time: 40 minutes

Serve: 2

Ingredients:

- 2/3 cup sushi rice;
- 1/2 carrot, cut into matchsticks;
- 2 nori sheets;
- 1 tbsp rice vinegar;
- 1/2 tsp soy sauce;
- 1/4 tsp liquid smoke;
- 1/2 tsp sesame oil;

- 1 tsp olive oil;
- 1/4 lb extra firm tofu;
- 3/4 cup water;
- 3/4 tsp salt.

Directions:

Add rice, water, and salt into the pot and bring to boil. Reduce heat and simmer for 20 minutes;

Transfer cooked rice into the bowl and add rice vinegar to the rice and mix well;

In an, another bowl, combine soy sauce, liquid smoke, sesame oil, and tofu;

Heat olive oil in a pan over medium heat;

Add marinated tofu in the pan and cook until golden brown on both the side;

Remove tofu from pan and set aside;

Place nori sheet on clean and plane surface;

Spread cooked rice evenly on nori sheet then place cooked tofu and carrot;

Slowly roll the nori sheet until you reach to another end of the roll;

Using a sharp knife cut the roll into the slices and serve.

Nutritional Value (Amount per Serving):

- **Calories** 480;
- **Fat** 13 g;
- **Carbohydrates** 77 g;
- **Protein** 20 g.

50-Fried Tofu Sushi

Time: 35 minutes

Serve: 10

Ingredients:

- 1 cup sushi rice; 1 tbsp sugar;
- 1 tsp salt;
- 1/8 cup rice vinegar; 1 cup water;
- 10 nori sheets;
- 1 block tofu, cut into cubes;
- 1/2 cup ginger, sliced;
- 2 avocados, sliced.

Directions:

Add rice, and water the pot and bring to boil. Reduce heat and simmer for 20 minutes;

Transfer cooked rice into the bowl;

Add rice vinegar, sugar, and salt into the pan and cook until sugar is dissolved;

Add vinegar mixture to the rice and mix well; Heat pan over medium heat;

Add tofu to the pan and cook until golden brown on both the sides;

Remove tofu pan from heat and set aside to cool; Place nori sheet on clean and plane surface; Spread cooked rice evenly on nori sheet then place avocado, ginger, and tofu on rice layer;

Roll nori sheet slowly around the ingredients until you reach to another end of the roll;

Cut roll into the slices and serve.

Nutritional Value (Amount per Serving):

- **Calories** 236;
- **Fat** 21 g;
- **Carbohydrates** 9 g;
- **Protein** 6 g.

51- Healthy Vegan Sushi Rolls

Time: 25 minutes

Serve: 4

Ingredients:

- 2 tsp rice vinegar;
- 1/2 tsp salt;
- 2 tsp sugar;
- 2 cups sushi rice; 3 tsp soy sauce;
- 1 avocado, cut into slices;
- 1 cucumber, cut into slices;
- 1 carrot, cut into strips;
- 1 pack tofu, cut into cubes; 5 nori sheets.

Directions:

Cook rice according to the packet instruction; Transfer cooked rice into the bowl;

Add 1 tsp sugar, salt, and rice vinegar into the rice and mix well;

In another bowl, mix together remaining sugar, soy sauce, and tofu;

Heat pan over medium heat;

Add marinated tofu into the pan and cook until golden brown on both the sides;

Place nori sheet on the clean and plain surface; Spread cooked rice evenly on the nori sheet; Place tofu, carrot, cucumber, and avocado on rice layer; Roll nori sheet around the ingredients tightly until you reach to another end of the roll;

Cut roll into the slices and serve.

Nutritional Value (Amount per Serving):

- **Calories** 450;
- **Fat** 8 g;
- **Carbohydrates** 88 g;
- **Protein** 9 g.

52- *Asparagus Tofu Sushi Rolls*

Time: 40 minutes

Serve: 1

Ingredients:

- 2 cups sushi rice;
- 1/2 tsp salt;
- 2 tbsp sugar;
- 1/4 cup rice vinegar;

- 2 garlic cloves, minced;
- 1 nori sheet;
- 1/2 tsp oyster sauce;
- 1 tbsp soy sauce;
- 1/2 lb tofu, cut into cubes;
- 3 asparagus stalks, trimmed.

Directions:

Cook rice according to the packet instruction;

Transfer cooked rice into the bowl;

Add sugar and rice vinegar to the rice and mix well;

In another bowl, mix together soy sauce, oyster sauce, garlic, tofu, and asparagus;

Heat pan over medium heat;

Add marinated tofu and asparagus into the pan and cook until tofu is golden brown on both the side;

Place nori sheet on the clean and plain surface; Spread cooked rice evenly on the nori sheet; Place cooked tofu and asparagus on rice layer;

Roll nori sheet slowly around the ingredients until you reach to another end of the roll;

Cut roll into the slices and serve.

Nutritional Value (Amount per Serving):

- **Calories** 410;
- **Fat** 3 g;
- **Carbohydrates** 87 g;
- **Protein** 8 g;
- **Cholesterol** 0 mg.

53-Quinoa Tofu Sushi Rolls

Time: 30 minutes

Serve: 6

Ingredients:

- 6 nori sheets;
- 2 bell peppers, cut into strips; 3 tbsp tamari;
- 2 tbsp sugar;
- 4 tbsp rice vinegar; 2 cups water;
- 1 cup quinoa;
- 2 tbsp sesame oil, toasted; 15 oz firm tofu, cut into slices.

Directions:

Add quinoa and water to the pot and bring to boil. Reduce heat to low and simmer for 15 minutes;

Heat sesame oil in the pan over medium heat;

Add 1 tbsp tamari and tofu into the pan and cook until tofu is golden brown on both the side;

Take one pan and heat remaining tamari, sugar, and rice vinegar into the pan until sugar is dissolved;

Add tamari and sugar mixture into the cooked quinoa and mix well;

Place nori sheet on the clean and plain surface;

Spread quinoa evenly on nori sheet then place tofu and bell pepper on rice layer;

Slowly roll the nori sheet around the ingredients until you reach the other end of the roll;

Cut roll into the slices and serve.

Nutritional Value (Amount per Serving):

- **Calories** 236;
- **Fat** 9 g;
- **Carbohydrates** 27 g;
- **Sugar** 6 g;
- **Protein** 11 g;

54-Tofu Brown Rice Sushi Rolls

Time: 25 minutes

Serve: 1

Ingredients:

- 1/3 cup Brown Rice;
- 1 tsp rice vinegar;
- 1/4 carrot, grated;
- 1/4 cup green lettuce;
- 3.5 oz tofu, fried and cut into strips;
- 1/2 tsp sugar;
- 1 nori sheets;
- 1/2 small red capsicum, cut into thin strips;
- 1/4 cucumber, cut into thin strips.

Directions:

Add 2/3 cup water and brown rice to the pot and bring to boil;

Reduce heat and simmer for 20 minutes;

In a small bowl, mix together vinegar and sugar;

Add vinegar and sugar mixture into the cooked rice and mix well;

Place nori sheet on the clean and plain surface;

Spread cooked rice on nori sheet evenly then place carrot, green lettuce, tofu, capsicum, and cucumber on rice layer; Roll nori sheet slowly around the ingredients until you reach to another end of the roll;

Cut roll into the slices and serve.

Nutritional Value (Amount per Serving):

- **Calories** 332;
- **Fat** 5.9 g;
- **Carbohydrates** 56 g;
- **Sugar** 4 g;
- **Protein** 14 g;
- **Cholesterol** 0 mg.

55-Smoked Tofu Avocado Sushi Rolls

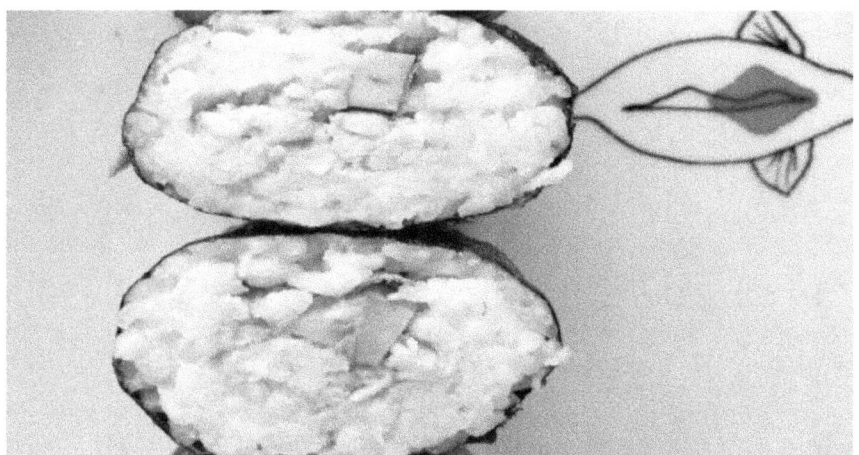

Time: 50 minutes

Serve: 4

Ingredients:

- 4 nori sheets;
- 6 oz smoked tofu, cut into strips;
- 1 cup sushi rice;
- 3 tbsp rice vinegar;
- 1 tsp salt;
- 1/2 avocado, sliced;
- 2 tsp sesame seeds.

Directions:

Cook sushi rice according to the packet instruction; Add vinegar and salt to the rice and mix well; Place nori sheet on the clean and plain surface;

Spread cooked rice evenly on nori sheet then place tofu, avocado, and sesame seeds on rice layer;

Roll nori sheet tightly around the ingredients until you reach the other end of the roll;

Cut roll into the slices and serve.

Nutritional Value (Amount per Serving):

- **Calories** 317;
- **Fat** 10 g;
- **Carbohydrates** 41 g;
- **Sugar** 0.2 g;
- **Protein** 12 g;
- **Cholesterol** 0 mg.

DID YOU KNOW?

15) There are Massive Limestone Caves

There is actually a huge amount of limestone caves strewn throughout the country and is a great way to escape the summer heat or winter cold since the temperature in the caves stays constant year-round.

These caves were formed millions of years ago and feature natural formations like limestone pools, streams, and underground waterfalls. A couple of the most famous limestone caves in Japan are Akiyoshido Cave, Abukumado Cave, and Ryusendo Cave.

16) You Can Find Beautiful Marshland in the Country

Japan has some of the most beautiful marshlands in the world that are especially popular to visit during the autumn months when the leaves change color. Hopefully, one day I can visit these marshlands during the fall colors as you get to see not only the leaves change colors, but also the grass in the marshland. A few of the most popular marshlands in Japan are Oze National Park, Senjogahara Marshland, and Kushiro Marshland.

17) Nachi – The Tallest Waterfall in Japan

Standing at a height of 133 meters, Nachi Falls is the tallest waterfall in Japan and is located in Nachikatsuura, Wakayama Prefecture. It is ranked as one of the three most beautiful and greatest waterfalls in Japan and is also part of the Kumano Kodo pilgrimage

Seafood Sushi Recipes

56-Salmon Sushi Rolls

Time: 40 minutes

Serve: 6

Ingredients:

- 4 oz sushi rice;
- 10 oz fresh salmon, cut into pieces; 1 avocado;
- 2 nori sheets;
- 3 tbsp sesame seeds; 1 tsp wasabi paste;
- 2 tbsp rice vinegar; 1/2 tbsp mirin;
- 1 tsp sugar; 1/2 tsp salt.

Directions:

Cook sushi rice according to the packet instruction;

In a pan heat rice vinegar, wasabi paste, mirin, sugar, and salt until sugar are dissolved;

Add vinegar mixture to the rice and mix well;

Place nori sheet on clean and plain surface and spread sushi rice evenly on the nori sheet;

Sprinkle sesame seeds on rice layer;

Arrange salmon and avocado on rice layer and roll nori sheet until you reach the other end of the roll;

Cut roll into the slices and serve.

Nutritional Value (Amount per Serving):

- **Calories** 260;
- **Fat** 14 g;
- **Carbohydrates** 21 g;
- **Protein** 13 g.

57- Smoked Salmon Sushi Rolls

Time: 40 minutes

Serve: 6

Ingredients:

- 2 tbsp wasabi paste;
- 8 oz smoked salmon, cut into strips; 1 cucumber, sliced;
- 1 avocado, sliced;
- 6 nori sheets;
- 6 tbsp rice wine vinegar; 2 cups sushi rice.

Directions:

Cook rice according to the packet instructions; Add vinegar to the rice and mix well;

Place nori sheet on the clean and plain surface;

Spread rice evenly on nori sheet then dot little wasabi paste on rice layer;

Place salmon, cucumber, and avocado on rice layer;

Roll nori sheet slowly around the ingredients until you reach to another end of the roll;

Cut roll into the slices and serve.

Nutritional Value (Amount per Serving):

- **Calories** 291;
- **Fat** 7 g;
- **Carbohydrates** 45 g;
- **Protein** 11 g;
- **Cholesterol** 9 mg.

58- Tuna Sushi Roll

Time: 55 minutes

Serve: 11

Ingredients:

- 4 oz tuna fillet, cut into pieces;
- 4 oz salmon fillet, cut into pieces;
- 2 2/3 cups sushi rice;
- 11 nori sheets;
- 14 oz imitation crab;
- 1 1/2 tsp sesame seeds;
- 3 1/2 tbsp rice vinegar; 1 avocado, sliced;
- 1 cucumber, cut into strips; 2 1/2 tbsp sugar;
- 1 1/2 tsp salt.

Directions:

Cook sushi rice according to the packet instructions; Add salt, sugar, and vinegar into the rice and mix well;

Place nori sheet on clean and plain surface and spread rice evenly on the nori sheet;

Sprinkle sesame seeds on rice layer;

Arrange tuna, salmon, crab, avocado, and cucumber on rice layer;

Roll nori sheet around the ingredients tightly until you reach the other end of the roll;

Cut roll into the slices and serve.

Nutritional Value (Amount per Serving):

- **Calories** 90;
- **Fat** 1 g;
- **Carbohydrates** 13 g;
- **Protein** 5 g.

59-Salmon Cauliflower Sushi Rolls

Time: 45 minutes

Serve: 3

Ingredients:

- 1/2 avocado, sliced;
- 5 oz smoked salmon, cut into pieces; 1 tbsp Rice Vinegar;
- 1 tbsp Soy Sauce; 5 nori sheets;

- 16 oz cauliflower;
- 6 oz Cream Cheese, softened; 1 cucumber, cut into strips.

Directions:

Add cauliflower rice into the food processor and process until it looks like rice;

Heat pan over medium heat add cauliflower rice and soy sauce into the pan and cook;

Once cauliflower rice is dried then add rice vinegar and cream cheese and mix well;

Remove cauliflower rice from heat and set aside to cool; Place nori sheet on clean and plane surface and spread cauliflower rice on the nori sheet;

Arrange cucumber, salmon, and avocado on cauliflower rice layer;

Roll nori sheet slowly around the ingredients tightly until you reach to another end of the sheet;

Cut roll into the slices and serve.

Nutritional Value (Amount per Serving):

- **Calories** 360;
- **Fat** 26 g;
- **Carbohydrates** 17 g;
- **Protein** 17 g.

60-Salmon Cream Cheese Sushi roll

Time: 25 minutes

Serve: 3

Ingredients:

- 3 nori sheets;
- 2 1/4 cup rice, cooked;
- 1 cucumber, cut into strips;
- 2 oz cream cheese, cut into strips;
- **3 oz salmon cut into strips.**

Directions:

Place nori sheet on clean and plane surface and spread rice on nori sheet evenly; Place cucumber, cream cheese, and salmon on rice layer; Slowly roll the nori sheet until you reach to another end of the sheet;

Cut roll into the slices and serve.

Nutritional Value (Amount per Serving):

- **Calories** 561;
- **Fat** 2 g;
- **Carbohydrates** 114 g;
- **Sugar** 1.9 g;
- **Protein** 16 g;
- **Cholesterol** 13 mg.

61-Salmon Sriracha Sushi Rolls

Time: 25 minutes

Serve: 3

Ingredients:

- 3 nori sheets;
- 2 1/4 cup cooked sushi rice; 1/2 avocado, sliced;
- 1 cucumber, cut into strips; 1/2 tsp sriracha chili sauce;
- 1 tbsp mayonnaise;
- 3 oz salmon, cut into pieces.

Directions:

In a bowl, add salmon, mayonnaise, and sriracha chili sauce and mix well;

Place nori sheet on clean and plain surface and spread rice evenly on sheet;

Arrange salmon, avocado, and cucumber on rice layer;

Roll nori sheet tightly around the ingredients until you reach the other end of the sheet;

Cut roll into the slices and serve.

Nutritional Value (Amount per Serving):

- **Calories** 648;
- **Fat** 11 g;
- **Carbohydrates** 1118 g;
- **Sugar** 2 g;

- **Protein** 17 g;
- **Cholesterol** 14 mg.

62- Canned Tuna Sushi Rolls

Time: 20 minutes

Serve: 4

Ingredients:

- 8 green onion, sliced; 1 cucumber, sliced;
- 1 avocado, sliced; 1 tbsp soy sauce;
- 2 tbsp mayonnaise;
- 1 can tuna;
- 2 cups cooked sushi rice; 4 nori sheets.

Directions:

In a bowl, mix together tuna, mayonnaise, and soy sauce; Place nori sheet on a clean surface;

Spread cooked rice evenly on the nori sheet;

Place green onion, cucumber, avocado, and tuna on rice layer;

Roll sheet tightly around the ingredients until you reach to another end of the sheet;

Cut roll into the slices and serve.

Nutritional Value (Amount per Serving):

- **Calories** 510;
- **Fat** 12 g;
- **Carbohydrates** 88 g;
- **Protein** 15 g.

63-Asparagus Crab Sushi Rolls

Time: 45 minutes

Serve: 6

Ingredients:

- 1 cup sushi rice;
- 2 tbsp mayonnaise;
- 6 nori sheets;
- 2 tbsp sushi Seasoning;
- 6 asparagus spears, trimmed cut into pieces;
- 8 oz fresh crab meat;
- 1 tbsp wasabi paste.

Directions:

Add rice and 1 1/2 cups water into the saucepan and bring to boil;

Reduce heat and simmer for 10 minutes;

In a bowl, combine mayonnaise, sushi seasoning, crab meat, and wasabi paste;

Place nori sheet on the plain and clean surface; Spread rice evenly on the nori sheet;

Place crab meat and asparagus on rice layer and roll nori sheet around the ingredients tightly until you reach to another end of the sheet;

Cut roll into the slices and serve.

Nutritional Value (Amount per Serving):

- **Calories** 320;
- **Fat** 4 g;
- **Carbohydrates** 49 g;
- **Protein** 17 g.

64- Spicy Cauliflower Tuna Sushi Rolls

Time: 45 minutes

Serve: 2

Ingredients:

- 1 large cauliflower head, cut into florets;
- 1 tbsp olive oil;
- 1/4 tsp salt;
- 2 nori sheets;
- 1/2 avocado, sliced;
- 1 cucumber, sliced;
- 2 tsp sriracha;
- 2 tbsp mayonnaise;

- 4 oz tuna.

Directions:

Preheat the oven to 425 F;

Add cauliflower florets into the food processor and process until it looks like rice;

Toss cauliflower rice with olive oil and salt and spread on a baking tray;

Toast cauliflower rice in preheated oven for 30 minutes; In a bowl, mix together tuna, mayonnaise, and sriracha; Place nori sheet on clean and plane surface;

Spread cauliflower rice on nori sheet then place tuna, avocado, and cucumber;

Roll nori wraps around the ingredients tightly until you reach to another end of the sheet;

Cut roll into the slices and serve.

Nutritional Value (Amount per Serving):

- **Calories** 480;
- **Fat** 23 g;
- **Carbohydrates** 52 g;
- **Protein** 26 g.

65-Delicious Shrimp Sushi Rolls

Time: 45 minutes

Serve: 4

Ingredients:

- 8 shrimps, cooked, peeled and cut into pieces;
- 1/2 avocado, sliced;
- 1 cucumber, cut into strips; 4 nori sheets;
- 1 1/2 cup water;
- 1 1/2 cup sushi rice; 1 tsp salt;
- 2 tsp sugar;
- 1/3 cup rice vinegar.

Directions:

Add rice, water, and salt into the saucepan and bring to boil. Reduce heat and simmer for 15 minutes;

Transfer cooked rice into the bowl to cool;

Add rice vinegar and sugar into the rice and mix well; Place nori sheet plain and clean surface;

Spread rice evenly on the nori sheet;

Place shrimp, avocado, and cucumber on rice layer; Slowly roll the nori sheet until you reach to another end of the sheet;

Cut roll into the slices and serve.

Nutritional Value (Amount per Serving):

- **Calories** 391;
- **Fat** 6 g;
- **Carbohydrates** 63 g;
- **Sugar** 3 g;
- **Protein** 16 g;
- **Cholesterol** 93 mg.

66- Spicy Tuna Sushi Rolls

Time: 1 hour 10 minutes

Serve: 5

Ingredients:

- 2 cups sushi rice;
- 1 avocado, cut into 2-inch pieces;
- 2 carrots, cut into 2-inch pieces;
- 5 nori sheets;
- ½ lb sashimi grade tuna, sliced into pieces;
- 5 tbsp sriracha chili sauce;
- ¼ tsp cumin powder;
- 1/8 tsp cayenne pepper;

- 1 tsp chili powder;
- ½ cup mayonnaise.

Directions:

In a small bowl, mix together mayonnaise, sriracha chili sauce, cumin powder, cayenne pepper, and chili powder. Set aside;

Cook sushi rice according to the packet instructions. Sushi rice should be sticky. Transfer rice in a bowl and place in a refrigerator for 30 minutes;

For sushi: place nori sheet on the bamboo mat then spread 1 cup cooked rice on nori evenly;

Place tuna in a line on 1/3 of the way up nori then followed by a line of avocado, cucumber, and carrot. Spread spicy mayonnaise mixture over the top;

Roll nori wrap tightly around ingredients until you reach the other end;

Cut the roll into ½ inch slices; Serve and enjoy.

Nutritional Value (Amount per Serving):

- **Calories** 528;
- **Fat** 16.7 g;
- **Carbohydrates** 77.3 g;
- **Sugar** 3 g;
- **Protein** 18.3 g;
- **Cholesterol** 6 mg.

67-Salmon Sushi Roll

Time: 15 minutes

Serve: 2

Ingredients:

- 2 sashimi salmon;
- 1 tbsp fresh lemon juice;
- ¼ avocado, cut into slices;
- 1 tbsp sesame seeds, toasted; 2 tbsp rice vinegar;
- 1 cup cooked sushi rice; 2 nori sheet.

Directions:

Add cooked rice, lemon juice, and vinegar in a large bowl and mix well;

Add sesame seeds and mix well;

For sushi: spread rice evenly on the nori sheet;

Arrange avocado slices and salmon on the sushi rice then roll nori sheet tightly around the ingredients until you reach to another end;

Cut into slices and serve.

Nutritional Value (Amount per Serving):

- **Calories** 485;
- **Fat** 15.7 g;
- **Carbohydrates** 64.4 g;
- **Sugar** 13.7 g;
- **Protein** 17.2 g;
- **Cholesterol** 0 mg.

68-Cucumber Salmon Sushi

Time: 30 minutes

Serve: 4

Ingredients:

- 1 ½ cups sushi rice;
- 5 oz sashimi grade salmon fillet, cut into 1/3" strips;
- ½ cucumber, sliced; 1 tsp wasabi paste; 4 nori sheet;
- 1 tbsp mirin;
- 1 tbsp sugar;
- ¼ cup rice vinegar;
- 1 tsp sea salt.

Directions:

Add rice and 1¾ cups water in a saucepan and bring to boil. Reduce heat and simmer for 12 minutes or until water is absorbed. Remove from heat and set aside;

In a small bowl, mix together vinegar, mirin, sugar, and salt until sugar is dissolved;

Transfer cooked rice in a large bowl. Add vinegar mixture to the rice and stir well;

Place nori sheet on bamboo mat. Spread ¼ of cooked rice on nori evenly;

Spread wasabi on rice then arrange ¼ of cucumber and salmon over wasabi;

Roll nori sheet tightly around the ingredients until you reach to another end;

Cut into slices and serve.

Nutritional Value (Amount per Serving):

- **Calories** 339;
- **Fat** 3.1 g;
- **Carbohydrates** 62 g;
- **Sugar** 4.7 g;
- **Protein** 12.6 g;
- **Cholesterol** 16 mg.

69-Tuna Teriyaki Rolls

Time: 15 minutes

Serve: 5

Ingredients:

- 5 nori sheets;
- 2 tsp sesame seeds, toasted;
- 3 tbsp teriyaki sauce;
- ½ lb sashimi grade tuna, cut into long strips; 1 tsp sugar;
- 1 tsp rice vinegar;
- 1 avocado, cut into slices;
- 2 ½ cups cooked sushi rice.

Directions:

In a bowl, add avocado, vinegar, and sugar and toss gently; Place nori sheet on bamboo mat;

Spread handful of cooked sushi rice on nori sheet evenly; Arrange tuna strips on rice then spoon teriyaki sauce over tuna;

Sprinkle with sesame seeds then arrange avocado slices; Roll nori sheet tightly around the ingredients until you reach to another end;

Cut into slices and serve.

Nutritional Value (Amount per Serving):

- **Calories** 490;
- **Fat** 9.5 g;
- **Carbohydrates** 80.5 g;
- **Sugar** 2.6 g;
- **Protein** 20 g;
- **Cholesterol** 0 mg.

70-Salmon Cream Cheese Roll

Time: 15 minutes

Serve: 4

Ingredients:

- 4 cups cooked sushi rice;
- ½ avocado, sliced into long strips;
- 1 cucumber, sliced into strips;
- 4 oz cream cheese, sliced into long strips;
- 5 oz sashimi grade salmon fillet, cut into 1/3" strips; 4 nori sheet.

Directions:

Place nori sheet on bamboo mat; Spread rice on nori sheet evenly;

Arrange salmon, avocado, cucumber, and cream cheese on top of rice;

Roll nori sheet tightly around the ingredients until you reach to another end;

Cut into slices and serve.

Nutritional Value (Amount per Serving):

- **Calories** 271;
- **Fat** 17.2 g;
- **Carbohydrates** 19.3 g;
- **Protein** 11.6 g;
- **Cholesterol** 47 mg.

71-Delicious Sashimi Tuna Roll

Time: 15 minutes

Serve: 4

Ingredients:

- 4 cups cooked sushi rice;
- ½ lb sashimi grade tuna, cut into long strips;
- ½ tsp chili powder; 1 tbsp mayonnaise;
- 1 tbsp sesame seeds, toasted;
- 4 nori sheets.

Directions:

In a small bowl, mix together mayonnaise and chili powder. Set aside;

Place nori sheet on top of the bamboo mat; Spread sushi rice on top of nori sheet evenly; Sprinkle sesame seed on top of sushi rice;

Arrange tuna on top of sushi rice then spread mayo mixture on top of tuna;

Roll nori sheet tightly around the ingredients until you reach to another end;

Cut into slices and serve.

Nutritional Value (Amount per Serving):

- **Calories** 378;
- **Fat** 7.3 g;
- **Carbohydrates** 55.3 g;
- **Sugar** 0.3 g;
- **Protein** 20.4 g;
- **Cholesterol** 19 mg.

72-New York Avocado Sushi

Time: 30 minutes

Serve: 6

Ingredients:

- 2 cups sushi rice;
- 1 cucumber, peeled and cut into julienne;
- 6 nori sheets;
- 24 shrimp, cooked, peeled and halved;

- 1 ½ tbsp fresh cilantro, chopped;
- 1 avocado, peeled and mashed;
- 1 tbsp wasabi;
- ¼ cup rice vinegar.

Directions:

Cook sushi rice according to the packet instruction. Remove from heat and stir in vinegar and set aside to cool;

In a small bowl, mix together avocado and wasabi and set aside;

In another small bowl, mix together shrimp and cilantro; Place nori sheet on a bamboo mat and spread rice evenly on nori;

Arrange cucumber, avocado, and shrimp on rice layer;

Roll nori sheet tightly around the ingredients until you reach to another end;

Cut into slices and serve.

Nutritional Value (Amount per Serving):

- **Calories** 414;
- **Fat** 8.5 g;
- **Carbohydrates** 55.7 g;
- **Sugar** 1.1 g;
- **Protein** 25.5 g;
- **Cholesterol** 185 mg.

73-Crab Meat Sushi

Time: 30 minutes

Serve: 24

Ingredients:

- 1 cup sushi rice;
- ¼ lb crab meat;
- ½ cucumber, peeled and cut in ¼ inch strips;
- 3 nori sheets;
- ½ avocado, sliced;
- 1 tsp dry sherry;
- 1 tsp sugar;
- 2 tbsp rice vinegar;
- ½ tsp salt.

Directions:

Cook sushi rice according to the packet instruction. Remove from heat and add sherry, sugar, rice vinegar and salt and stir well to combine;

Place nori sheet on a bamboo mat and spread sushi rice evenly on nori;

Arrange cucumber, avocado, and crab meat on rice layer; Roll nori sheet tightly around the ingredients until you reach to another end;

Cut into slices and serve.

Nutritional Value (Amount per Serving):

- **Calories** 43;
- **Fat** 1 g;
- **Carbohydrates** 7 g;
- **Sugar** 0.3 g;
- **Protein** 1.3 g;
- **Cholesterol** 3 mg.

74- Cucumber Crabmeat Sushi and Avocado

Time: 25 minutes

Serve: 8

Ingredients:

- 2/3 cup sushi rice;
- ½ lb imitation crabmeat, flakes; 1 avocado, sliced;
- 2 tbsp ginger, sliced;
- ½ cucumber, peeled and sliced; 4 nori sheets;
- 3 tbsp sugar;
- 3 tbsp rice vinegar; 1 ½ tsp salt.

Directions:

Cook rice according to the packet instructions. Remove from heat and add vinegar, salt, and sugar and stir well to combine;

Place nori sheet on a bamboo mat and spread rice evenly on nori;

Arrange avocado, ginger, cucumber, and crabmeat on rice layer;

Roll nori sheet tightly around the ingredients until you reach to another end;

Cut into slices and serve.

Nutritional Value (Amount per Serving):

- **Calories** 163;
- **Fat** 5.2 g;
- **Carbohydrates** 24.9 g;
- **Sugar** 6.8 g;
- **Protein** 4 g;
- **Cholesterol** 6 mg.

75- Flavorful Tuna Sushi Rolls

Time: 15 minutes

Serve: 2

Ingredients:

- ½ avocado, cut into thin strips;
- ½ cucumber, cut into strips;

- 1 can tuna;
- 2 nori sheets;
- 2 tbsp rice vinegar;
- 1 ½ cup cooked sushi rice.

Directions:

Add rice vinegar in sushi rice and mix well;

Place nori sheet on a bamboo mat and spread cooked sushi rice evenly on nori;

Arrange avocado, cucumber, and tuna on rice layer;

Roll nori sheet tightly around the ingredients until you reach to another end;

Cut into slices and serve.

Nutritional Value (Amount per Serving):

- **Calories** 471;
- **Fat** 17.3 g;
- **Carbohydrates** 47.1 g;
- **Sugar** 1.5 g;
- **Protein** 28.3 g;
- **Cholesterol** 28 mg.

DID YOU KNOW?

18) The 2003 Pet Boom of Japan

Starting around 2003, pets became more and more popular in Japan and by the year 2009, there were close to 6 million more cats and dogs than children in Japan.

This boom also has a reported dark side, though, as many people who were not 100% ready for a pet in their life decided to get one, and then shortly after decided the pet was too much and gave it to a shelter.

Because of this in 2010 a reported 500,000 dogs were put to death in public animal management centers in Japan.

19) Japanese Trains are Extremely Punctual

Trains in Japan are so punctual that it's scary! At the same time, it makes me wonder in awe how they do it because there are so many different train lines that run throughout the country on a given day.

In fact, in 2017, the Tsukuba Express line between Tokyo and Tsukuba made global headlines when the management of the train line apologized publicly for leaving the station 20 seconds early

20) Hikikomori – A Population Who has Withdrawn from Society

There is a population of mostly men in Japan, known as Hikikomori who have completely withdrawn from society and for the most part, haven't left their rooms for at least 6 months to 1 year. In the 2016 Japanese census, they counted about 540,000 people who would be considered Hikikomori, but it's hard to say because most of these people tend to want to stay under the radar. Even though the term is Japanese, there are Hikikomori in other parts of the world too, like the US, Brazil, and Oman.

Sashimi Recipes

76-Miso Soy Tuna Sashimi

Time: 15 minutes

Serve: 4

Ingredients:

- 12 oz sushi grade tuna, sliced thinly;
- ½ tsp wasabi paste;
- 2 tbsp soy sauce;
- 1 tsp miso;
- ½ fresh lemon juice;
- 2 tbsp olive oil.

Directions:

In a small bowl, whisk together oil, wasabi, soy sauce, and lemon juice;

Place tuna in a dish. Pour oil mixture over the tuna and let sit for 10-15 minutes;

Serve and enjoy.

Nutritional Value (Amount per Serving):

- **Calories** 229;
- **Fat** 14.2 g;
- **Carbohydrates** 1.2 g;
- **Sugar** 0.4 g;
- **Protein** 23.3 g;
- **Cholesterol** 26 mg.

77-Chive Soy Tuna Sashimi

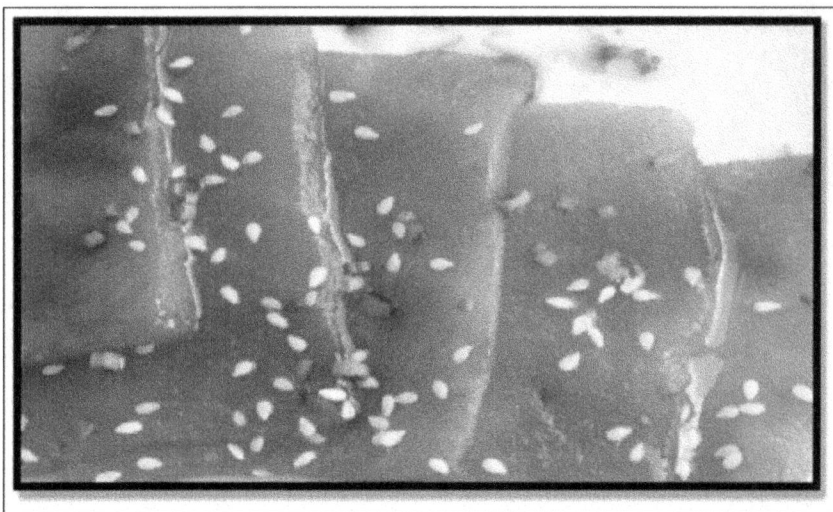

Time: 10 minutes

Serve: 8

Ingredients:

- 1 lb fresh sashimi quality tuna, sliced thinly;
- ½ tsp chives, sliced;
- 2 tsp sesame seeds, toasted;
- 4 tsp Shiro dashi;
- 2 tsp olive oil;

Directions:

Arrange sliced fish on a dish;

In a small bowl, mix together olive oil and Shiro dashi;

Drizzle olive oil mixture over sliced fish;

Sprinkle with chives and sesame seeds; Serve and enjoy.

Nutritional Value (Amount per Serving):

- **Calories** 120;
- **Fat** 6.1 g;
- **Carbohydrates** 0.2 g;
- **Sugar** 0 g;
- **Protein** 15.2 g;
- **Cholesterol** 18 mg.

78-Salmon Sashimi

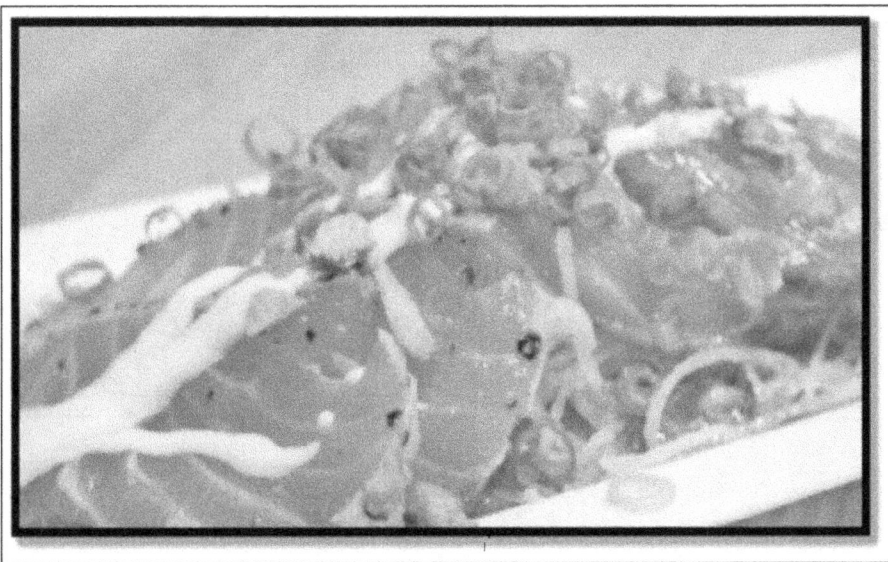

Time: 20 minutes

Serve: 4

Ingredients:

- ¾ lb salmon fillets, boneless and skin off;
- 1 spring onion, shredded;
- ¼ cup fresh coriander, chopped;
- 2 radishes, sliced thinly and cut into julienne;
- 1 baby carrot, shredded;

For dressing:

- 1 red chili, chopped;
- 1 ginger piece, sliced and cut into julienne;
- 1 tsp sesame oil;
- 2 tsp mirin;
- 1 tbsp rice vinegar;
- ¼ cup fresh lemon juice;
- ¼ cup soy sauce.

Directions:

In a small bowl, whisk together all dressing ingredients; Toss dressing with carrot and radish and leave to marinate for 10 minutes;

Meanwhile, sliced the salmon thinly using a sharp knife; Arrange salmon on serving dish and top with marinated veggies and dressing;

Garnish with spring onion and coriander; Serve and enjoy.

Nutritional Value (Amount per Serving):

- **Calories** 144;
- **Fat** 6.5 g;
- **Carbohydrates** 3.3 g;
- **Sugar** 1.5 g;
- **Protein** 17.8 g;
- **Cholesterol** 38 mg.

79-Ginger Salmon Sashimi

Time: 15 minutes

Serve: 4

Ingredients:

- ¾ lb salmon fillet, boneless, skin off and sliced thinly;
- 2 tbsp cilantro leaves;
- 1 ½ tsp sesame seeds, toasted; 1 tsp sesame oil;
- 2 tbsp grapeseed oil;
- 1 tbsp chives, chopped;
- 1 ginger piece, sliced and cut into julienne;
- 1 tsp fresh orange juice;
- 1 tsp fresh lime juice; 6 tbsp soy sauce.

Directions:

In a small bowl, mix together orange juice, lime juice, and 2 tbsp soy sauce;

In another bowl, toss salmon with remaining soy sauce and let sit for 1-2 minutes;

Arrange salmon slices on dish and top with chives and ginger;

Heat sesame oil and grapeseed oil in a small saucepan over high heat for 2 minutes;

Drizzle hot oil over sliced salmon. Spoon the orange juice mixture on top;

Garnish with cilantro leaves and sprinkle with sesame seeds;

Serve and enjoy.

Nutritional Value (Amount per Serving):

- **Calories** 138;
- **Fat** 7 g;
- **Carbohydrates** 1.7 g;
- **Sugar** 0.4 g;
- **Protein** 17.7 g;
- Cholesterol 38 mg.

80-Healthy Tuna Sashimi

Time: 15 minutes

Serve: 4

Ingredients:

- 6 oz sashimi grade tuna;
- 1 tbsp prepared wasabi;
- 1 tsp sesame seeds, toasted;
- 1 tsp fresh chili paste;
- ¼ tsp sesame oil;

- ¼ cup soy sauce;
- 1 tbsp green onion, sliced.

Directions:

Sliced tuna using a sharp knife; Arrange sliced tuna on a dish;

In a small bowl, whisk together wasabi, chili paste, sesame oil, and soy sauce;

Drizzle sauce mixture over sliced tuna;

Garnish with green onion and sprinkle with sesame seeds; Serve and enjoy.

Nutritional Value (Amount per Serving):

- **Calories** 99;
- **Fat** 4.3 g;
- **Carbohydrates** 2 g;
- Protein 12.5 g;
- **Cholesterol** 14 mg.

81-Sea Bass Sashimi

Time: 15 minutes

Serve: 4

Ingredients:

- 1 lb sashimi grade sea bass fillets, skin off and sliced thinly;
- 1 orange, segmented;

- 2 tbsp sesame seeds, toasted; 1 fresh red chili, chopped;
- 1 kaffir lime leaf, shredded;
- 1 tbsp fresh ginger, grated;
- 1 tbsp sesame oil;
- 1 tbsp fish sauce;
- 2 tbsp fresh orange juice;
- 2 tbsp soy sauce.

Directions:

Arrange sliced dish on the dish;

In a small bowl, whisk together soy sauce, sesame seeds, chili, lime leaf, ginger, sesame oil, fish sauce, and orange juice;

Arrange orange segments over fish; Drizzle sliced fish with dressing and serve.

Nutritional Value (Amount per Serving):

- **Calories** 232;
- **Fat** 8.7 g;
- **Carbohydrates** 9 g;
- **Sugar** 5.3 g;
- **Protein** 28.9 g;
- **Cholesterol** 60 mg.

82-Delicious Tuna Sashimi

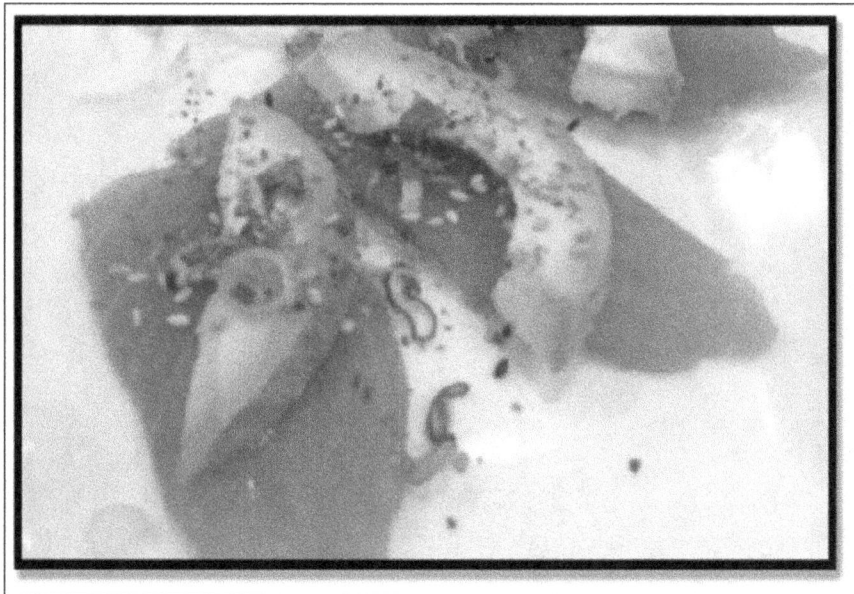

Time: 10 minutes

Serve: 6

Ingredients:

- 1 lb sashimi grade tuna, sliced thinly;
- ½ cup soy sauce;
- 4 spring onions, sliced;
- 1 tbsp fresh lime juice;
- 2 tbsp olive oil;
- 2 avocados, cut into thick slices.

Directions:

Arrange tuna and avocado slices on a dish;

Mix together lime juice and olive oil and pour over sliced tuna and avocado;

Garnish with spring onion and serve with soy sauce.

Nutritional Value (Amount per Serving):

- **Calories** 332;
- **Fat** 23.9 g;
- **Carbohydrates** 8.1 g;
- **Sugar** 0.9 g;
- **Protein** 22.8 g;
- **Cholesterol** 23 mg.

DID YOU KNOW?

21) Mount Takao: A Natural Recreation Area Near Tokyo

If you're spending time in Tokyo, you actually don't need to go too far in order to get into the mountains of Japan! Mount Takao (高尾山, Takaosan) is located only 50 minutes away from Shinjuku Station and will only set you back about ¥ 390.

Once you get there, you can hike up to the summit which is close to 2,000 feet or if you don't feel like hiking the whole way, you can also take the cable car which brings you halfway up the mountain.

From the top, you can see views of Tokyo, and on clear days you can even see Mount Fuji!

22) Japan has Sand Dunes

Yes, surprisingly Japan also has a dune, which means they pretty much have everything you would ever want in a country! All jokes aside, the largest and only dune in the country is the Tottori Sand Dunes which is 9 miles long and 1.5 miles wide.

Over 2 million visitors come here annually to explore the dunes. There are also other activities here to take part in too like sandboarding, paragliding, camel rides, a museum to visit, and even taking the chairlift up to an observation deck.

23) There was a Ban on Dancing After Midnight

Interestingly, there was a ban in Japan on dancing after midnight or 1 am in bars, clubs, and other public venues that lasted from 1948 to 2015. This law was first put into place during WWII because many of the dancing venues during the US occupation of Japan was actually a front for prostitution.

24) The Country has a Huge Number of Onsens

Because of Japan's geographic location and its volcanic activity, the country has about 2,300 Onsens to choose from located all around the country. It is said that the water from these hot springs can treat a variety of things including rheumatism, hypertension, fatigue, and chronic skin conditions like eczema.

I was lucky enough to have stayed at a ryokan in the Lake Kawaguchiko area so I got to experience a private Onsen while I was there. Hopefully, I can make it to some other Onsens on my next visits to Japan as I've always wanted to try the ones in Hakone out.

Nigiri Sushi

83-Fresh Tuna Nigiri Sushi

Time: 20 minutes

Serve: 16

Ingredients:

- 1 cup sushi rice;
- ½ nori sheet, cut into half-inch strips;
- 5 oz sushi grade tuna, sliced thinly;
- 1 tsp rice vinegar.

Directions:

Cook sushi rice to the packet direction. Once cooked remove from heat and set aside to cool;

Dip fingers in rice vinegar and water and give the shape 1 ½ tablespoon rice into a rectangle;

Place tuna slice over rice rectangle and wrap nori strip around tuna and rice to seal;

Repeat same with remaining ingredients; Serve and enjoy.

Nutritional Value (Amount per Serving):

- **Calories** 54;
- **Fat** 0.6 g;
- **Carbohydrates** 9.3 g;
- **Sugar** 0 g;
- **Protein** 2.6 g;
- **Cholesterol** 4 mg.

84- Salmon Nigiri Sushi

Time: 45 minutes

Serve: 4

Ingredients:

- 3 oz salmon fillets, skinless;
- ¼ tsp sugar;
- 1 tbsp rice vinegar;
- 1 ½ cup water;
- 1 cup sushi rice;
- ¼ tsp salt.

Directions:

Add rice and water in a large saucepan and bring to boil over medium heat. Reduce heat to low and simmer for 5 minutes;

Remove saucepan from heat and set aside for 15 minutes;

Transfer rice in a large bowl. Add vinegar, sugar, and salt to the rice and mix well;

Slice salmon in 8 slices;

Take 1 tbsp cooked rice into hands and roll in a ball. Wrap fish slice over rice and arrange on serving dish;

Repeat same with remaining ingredients; Serve and enjoy.

Nutritional Value (Amount per Serving):

- **Calories** 200;
- **Fat** 1.6 g;
- **Carbohydrates** 37.2 g;
- **Sugar** 0.3 g;
- **Protein** 7.4 g;
- **Cholesterol** 9 mg.

85- Shrimp Nigiri

Time: 20 minutes

Serve: 12

Ingredients:

- 1 ¼ cup cooked sushi rice;
- 1 tsp wasabi;
- 12 shrimp, cooked, peel and leave the tails on.

Directions:

Divide sushi rice into 12 equal portions and shape each portion into a rectangle with moistened hands;

Brush shrimp with wasabi and place on rice rectangle; Serve and enjoy.

Nutritional Value (Amount per Serving):

- **Calories** 97;
- **Fat** 0.5 g;
- **Carbohydrates** 15.8 g;
- **Protein** 6.4 g;
- **Cholesterol** 46 mg.

86- Scallop Nigiri

Time: 15 minutes

Serve: 2

Ingredients:

- 2 sushi-grade scallops;
- 2 tsp rice vinegar;
- ¼ cup water;
- 1/3 cup cooked sushi rice.

Directions:

Cut the muscle from scallops and butterfly the scallops; Moistened your hands with water vinegar and take 1 tablespoon of cooked sushi rice and give it a rectangular shape and place on a dish;

Place scallops on rice and serve.

Nutritional Value (Amount per Serving):

- **Calories** 142;
- **Fat** 0.4 g;
- **Carbohydrates** 25.4 g;
- **Sugar** 0 g;
- **Protein** 7.2 g;
- **Cholesterol** 10 mg.

87- Avocado Nigiri

Time: 50 minutes

Serve: 16

Ingredients:

- 1 avocado, peel and cut into sliced;
- 1 nori sheet, cut into strips;
- 1 tsp sugar;
- ½ tbsp rice vinegar;
- 1 cup water;
- 1 cup sushi rice;
- 1 tsp salt.

Directions:

Cook sushi rice according to the packet instructions; Transfer cooked rice in a large bowl and allow to cool;

Once rice is cool down then add vinegar, sugar, and salt and mixes well;

Moistened your hands with water and take 1 tablespoon of cooked sushi rice and give it a rectangular shape and place on a dish;

Place an avocado slice over rice rectangle and wrap nori strip around avocado and rice to seal;

Repeat same with remaining ingredients; Serve and enjoy.

Nutritional Value (Amount per Serving):

- **Calories** 69;
- **Fat** 2.5 g;
- **Carbohydrates** 10.6 g;
- **Sugar** 0.3 g;
- **Protein** 1.1 g;
- **Cholesterol** 0 mg.

88-Tasty Hamachi Nigiri

Time: 15 minutes

Serve: 10

Ingredients:

- 4.5 oz hamachi fillet, sliced into thin strips;
- 10 shiso cress leaves;
- 1 1/4 cup cooked sushi rice;
- 1 tsp sugar;
- 1 tsp rice vinegar;
- ¼ tsp salt.

Directions:

Transfer cooked rice in a large bowl. Add sugar, vinegar, and salt to the rice and mix well;

Divide sushi rice into 10 equal portions and shape each portion into a rectangle with moistened hands;

Place hamachi slices on top of rice;

Garnish each nigiri with shiso leaves and serve.

Nutritional Value (Amount per Serving):

- **Calories** 105;
- **Fat** 0.8 g;
- **Carbohydrates** 18.9 g;
- **Sugar** 0.4 g;
- **Protein** 4.6 g;
- **Cholesterol** 7 mg.

89- Cucumber Nigiri

Time: 20 minutes

Serve: 16

Ingredients:

- 1 cup sushi rice;
- 1/2 nori sheet, cut into half-inch strips;
- 1 cucumber, peeled and sliced thinly;
- 1 tsp rice vinegar.

Directions:

Cook sushi rice to the packet direction. Once cooked remove from heat and set aside to cool;

Dip fingers in rice vinegar and water and give the shape 1 ½ tablespoon rice into a rectangle;

Place cucumber slice over rice rectangle and wrap nori strip around cucumber and rice to seal;

Repeat same with remaining ingredients;

Serve and enjoy.

Nutritional Value (Amount per Serving):

- **Calories** 45;
- **Fat** 0.1 g;
- **Carbohydrates** 9.9 g;
- **Protein** 0.9 g.

90-Healthy Carrot Nigiri

Time: 25 minutes

Serve: 10

Ingredients:

- 2 carrots, peeled;
- 2 cups cooked sushi rice;
- ¼ cup white wine.

Directions:

Pour white wine in a saucepan;

Add carrot in a saucepan and heat over medium heat for 3-5 minutes or until carrot is tender. Remove from heat and set aside to cool;

Once the carrot is cool then sliced;

Divide sushi rice into 10 equal portions and shape each portion into a rectangle with moistened hands;

Place carrot slices on top of rice;

Serve and enjoy.

Nutritional Value (Amount per Serving):

- **Calories** 145;
- **Fat** 0.2 g;
- **Carbohydrates** 30.9 g;
- **Protein** 2.7 g.

DID YOU KNOW?

25) Only 1.7% of Land in Japan is Pastures and Grassland

When you think about it, this isn't really that surprising, yet it surprised me. I would have thought the Japanese countryside would have more grassland, but because the country is so mountainous, forested and the cities so developed, pastures and grassland only make up a small proportion of the country's geography.

26) One of the Lowest Unemployment Rates in the World

Although the work-life balance in Japan isn't the best, the country does have one of the lowest unemployment rates in the entire world. The current unemployment rate in the country is 2.4%, which isn't so low when you compare it to Cambodia and Qatar which have an unemployment rate of 0.30% and 0.60%. However, when you compare it to the world's largest economies like the US, China, Germany, and the United Kingdom, you get a sense of how low it is.

Unemployment Rate in the World's Largest Economies:

- Japan 2.3%
- China 3.67%
- United States 3.8%
- United Kingdom 3.8%

27) Oldest Company in the World Until 2006

Kongo Gumi Co. Ltd, an Osaka founded and based construction company that specialized in building Buddhist temples was actually the oldest running company with over 1,400 years of history before it was purchased and absorbed by the Takamatsu Construction Group in 2006.

28) Japan Just Legalized Gambling Casinos

While gambling was illegal in Japan for several years, on July 20, 2018, it was legalized in the form of gambling casinos. Even though gambling was illegal for that long of a time, people in Japan were still able to "gamble" in the form of Pachinko, which looks like the craziest game of pinball you can ever play. To get around the illegal gambling law, at the Pachinko Parlor, you would trade in metal balls that you win for some sort of token and then take a short walk to a location nearby to trade in that token for cash.

Dessert Sushi Recipes

91-Yummy Banana Nutella Sushi Roll

Time: 15 minutes

Serve: 2

Ingredients:

- 2 bananas, peeled;
- 4 tbsp Nutella;
- 2 tortillas bread.

Directions:

Place tortilla on a plain surface and spread Nutella on a tortilla;

Place banana on tortilla and roll tortilla around the banana tightly;

Cut roll into the slices and serve.

Nutritional Value (Amount per Serving):

- **Calories** 357;
- **Fat** 13 g;
- **Carbohydrates** 58 g;
- **Sugar** 35 g;
- **Protein** 4 g;
- **Cholesterol** 0 mg.

92- Chocolate Fruit Sushi Rolls

Time: 45 minutes

Serve: 8

Ingredients:

- 1 1/2 oz strawberries, sliced;
- 1 1/2 oz kiwi, sliced;
- 1/3 cup chocolate chips, melted; 1 tbsp milk;
- 1/2 cup sushi rice;
- 1 1/3 cups coconut milk; 6 tbsp sugar;
- 1/4 tsp vanilla extract; 2 tbsp cocoa powder;
- 5 tbsp all-purpose flour; 1/2 tsp salt;
- 2 tbsp butter, softened.

Directions:

Add rice, 1/4 tsp salt, 2 tbsp sugar, and coconut milk into the pot and bring to boil;

Reduce heat and simmer for 20 minutes;

In a medium bowl, mix together remaining sugar and butter until creamy;

Add cocoa powder, vanilla, and milk and mix until smooth; Stir in all-purpose flour and remaining salt;

Place waxed paper on plain surface and roll chocolate dough into the middle of the large sheet;

Spread rice evenly on chocolate dough and place sliced kiwi and strawberries;

Roll chocolate dough slowly around the ingredients until you reach to another end of the rolled dough;

Using a sharp knife cut the roll into the slices; Serve with melted chocolate and enjoy.

Nutritional Value (Amount per Serving):

- **Calories** 260;
- **Fat** 15 g;
- **Carbohydrates** 31 g;
- **Protein** 3 g.

93- Fresh Fruit Sushi Rolls

Time: 45 minutes

Serve: 5

Ingredients:

- 1 1/2 cups sushi rice, uncooked;
- 1/4 tsp salt;
- 1/2 cup sugar;
- 14 oz coconut milk;
- 2 1/4 cup water;
- 5 fruit rolls;
- 1 cup fresh strawberries, sliced;

- 1 kiwi, sliced;
- 1 mango, sliced.

Directions:

Add rice and water to the pot and bring to boil. Reduce heat and simmer for 20 minutes;

In a saucepan, add sugar, coconut milk, and salt and bring to boil;

Once it starts boiling then removes from heat and stir into cooked rice;

Set rice aside to cool;

Place fruit roll on the plain and clean surface and spread cooked rice evenly on a roll;

Arrange fruits on rice and layer and slowly roll until you reach to another end of the roll;

Cut roll into the slices and serve.

Nutritional Value (Amount per Serving):

- **Calories** 519;
- **Fat** 19 g;
- **Carbohydrates** 83 g;
- **Protein** 6 g.

94-Banana Nuts Sushi

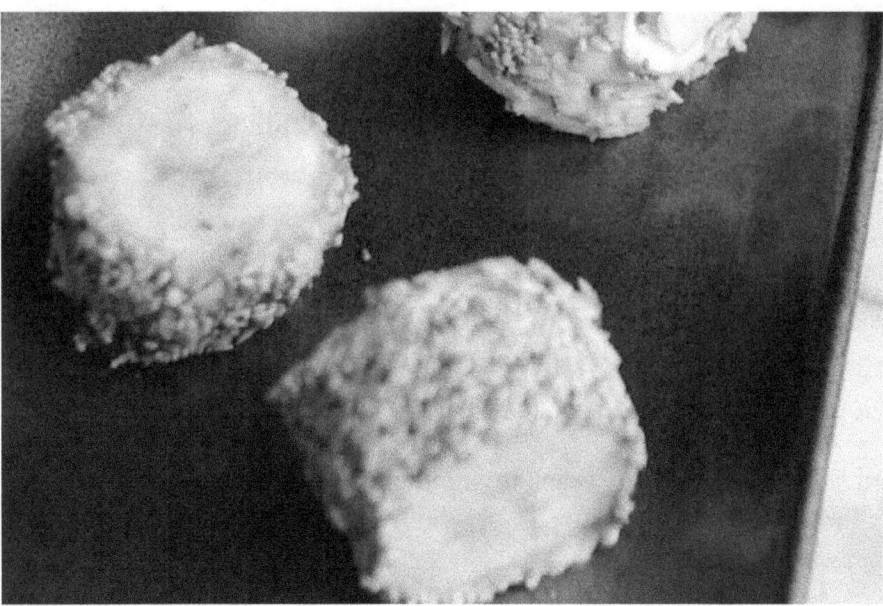

Time: 15 minutes

Serve: 2

Ingredients:

- 1/3 cup nuts, crushed;
- 2 tbsp. almond butter, unsweetened;
- 1 banana, peeled.

Directions:

Spread almond butter on a banana; Place crushed nuts in a shallow dish; Roll banana in crushed nuts;

Cut banana into slices and serve.

Nutritional Value (Amount per Serving):

- **Calories** 290;
- **Fat** 20 g;
- **Carbohydrates** 22 g;
- **Protein** 10 g.

95-Sweet and Spicy Grapefruit Sushi Rolls

Time: 55 minutes

Serve: 8

Ingredients:

- 1/4 cup grapefruit Juice
- 1 tsp grapefruit zest
- 1/8 cup white wine
- 1/8 tsp powdered wasabi
- 2 grapefruit, peeled and sliced
- 4 nori sheets
- 1 tsp sugar
- 3 cups water
- 2 cups sushi rice
- 1/2 cup rice vinegar
- 1/8 cup sugar
- 1 tbsp sweet chili Sauce
- 1 tbsp olive oil
- 1 tsp salt

Directions:

Add rice and water to the saucepan and bring to boil. Reduce heat and simmer for 20 minutes.

In a small saucepan, add olive oil, salt, sugar, and vinegar and boil until sugar is dissolved. Remove from heat and set aside.

Add olive oil mixture to the rice and mix well.

Add 1 grapefruit, wasabi, chili sauce, sugar, white wine, grapefruit juice, and zest into the blender and blend until smooth. Pour into the bowl and place in refrigerator.

Place nori sheet on clean and plain surface.

Spread rice evenly on nori sheet then place sliced grapefruit on rice layer.

Roll nori sheet slowly around the ingredients well.

Cut roll into the slices and serve with chilled sweet and spicy grapefruit sauce.

Nutritional Value (Amount per Serving):

- **Calories** 250
- **Fat** 2 g
- **Carbohydrates** 52 g
- **Protein** 5 g

96-Chia Honey Banana Sushi Rolls

Time: 20 minutes

Serve: 4

Ingredients:

- 1 tbsp poppy seeds;
- 1 tbsp chia seeds;
- 1 tbsp honey;
- 1 banana, peeled.

Directions:

In a shallow dish, mix together chia seeds and poppy seeds;

Spread honey on peeled banana then rolls banana into the chia and poppy seed;

Cut banana roll into the slices and serve.

Nutritional Value (Amount per Serving):

- **Calories** 70;
- **Fat** 2 g;
- **Carbohydrates** 12 g;
- **Protein** 1 g.

97-Yummy Mango Sushi

Time: 30 minutes

Serve: 1

Ingredients:

- 2 cups sushi rice, cooked;
- 1 nori sheet;
- 1 mango, sliced;
- 1/2 tsp lime juice;
- 1/4 tsp salt;
- 1 tsp sugar;
- 3 tbsp coconut milk.

Directions:

Add lime juice, salt, sugar, and coconut milk into the rice and mix well;

Place nori sheet on clean and plain surface and spread rice evenly on sheet;

Place mango slices on rice layer and roll nori sheet slowly until you reach the other end of the sheet; Cut roll into the slices and serve.

Nutritional Value (Amount per Serving):

- **Calories** 1620;
- **Fat** 14 g;
- **Carbohydrates** 346 g;
- **Protein** 29 g.

98- Gluten Free Chocó Oats Banana Sushi

Time: 20 minutes

Serve: 2

Ingredients:

- 1 cup chocolate honey oats;
- 1 tbsp almond butter;
- 1 banana, peeled;

Directions:

Crush the oats and place into the shallow dish;

Spread almond butter on banana then rolls the banana in crushed oats;

Cut banana roll into the slices and serve;

Nutritional Value (Amount per Serving):

- **Calories** 620;
- **Fat** 4 g;
- **Carbohydrates** 154 g;
- **Protein** 2 g.

99-Yummy Strawberry Jam Sushi

Time: 15 minutes

Serve: 1

Ingredients:

- 2 bread slices;
- 2 tbsp strawberry jam;
- 2 tbsp creamy peanut butter.

Directions:

Cut the crust of bread slices;

Using rolling pin flatten the bread completely;

Spread 1 tbsp jam and peanut butter on each slice;

Roll each bread slices and cut into pieces;

Serve and enjoy.

Nutritional Value (Amount per Serving):

- **Calories** 423;
- **Fat** 17 g;
- **Carbohydrates** 58 g;
- **Protein** 11 g.

100- Chocolate Walnut Banana Sushi

Time: 20 minutes

Serve: 4

Ingredients:

- 2 whole wheat tortillas;
- 2 tbsp coconut powder;
- 2 tbsp walnut, chopped;
- 4 tbsp Nutella;
- 2 bananas, peeled.

Directions:

Place tortilla on a plain surface and spread Nutella on a tortilla;

Sprinkle chopped walnuts and coconut powder;

Place peeled banana on tortilla and roll tightly around the banana;

Cut roll into the slices and serve.

Nutritional Value (Amount per Serving):

- **Calories** 240;
- **Fat** 10 g;
- **Carbohydrates** 36 g;
- **Protein** 3 g.

101- Pineapple Cantaloupe Strawberry Sushi Rolls

Time: 40 minutes

Serve: 16

Ingredients:

- 2 cups sushi rice;
- 1/2 pineapple, peeled and cut into pieces;
- 1/2 cantaloupe, cut into pieces;
- 16 fresh strawberries, quartered;
- 16 soy wrappers;
- 1 tbsp coconut cream.

Directions:

Cook rice according to the packet instruction and set aside to cool;

Stir coconut cream in cooked rice;

Place soy wrapper on the clean and plain surface; Spread 1/4 cup sushi rice evenly on soy wrapper;

Arrange fruits on rice layer and roll wrapper tightly around the ingredients until you reach to another end of the wrapper;

Cut roll into the slices and serve.

Nutritional Value (Amount per Serving):

- **Calories** 122;
- **Fat** 0.9 g;
- **Carbohydrates** 23.5 g;
- **Protein** 3.9 g.

www.ingramcontent.com/pod-product-compliance
Lightning Source LLC
Chambersburg PA
CBHW081348080526
44588CB00016B/2418